AMY'S
BAKING YEAR

For my mum, Gillian.

AMY'S BAKING YEAR

SEASONAL RECIPES FROM BRITAIN'S YOUNGEST BAKER

Amy-Beth Ellice

metro

Published by Metro Publishing
an imprint of John Blake Publishing Ltd
3 Bramber Court, 2 Bramber Road,
London W14 9PB, England

www.johnblakepublishing.co.uk

www.facebook.com/johnblakebooks ⬦
twitter.com/jblakebooks ⬦

First published in hardback in 2014

ISBN: 978-1-78219-997-7

British Library Cataloguing-in-Publication Data:

A catalogue record for this book is available from the British Library.

Design: www.envydesign.co.uk
Home economy: Amy-Beth Ellice
Food styling: Amy-Beth Ellice
Props styling: Charlotte Love
Photography: Joanna Henderson
Lace image: Shutterstock

Printed and bound by Polestar Wheatons Ltd, Exeter

1 3 5 7 9 10 8 6 4 2

Papers used by John Blake Publishing are natural, recyclable products made from wood
grown in sustainable forests. The manufacturing processes conform to the
environmental regulations of the country of origin.

Every attempt has been made to contact the relevant copyright-holders, but some
were unobtainable. We would be grateful if the appropriate people could contact us.

About the Author

Amy-Beth Ellice is sixteen years old and has grown up in a creative family in a small village in Essex. The kitchen being the heart of the home, Amy developed a passion for cooking and baking from an exceptionally young age inspired by her mum Gillian along with the TV cooks whom she loves to watch, such as Nigella Lawson and Ina Garten. Amy has been involved in cooking healthy everyday meals and baking homemade treats for special occasions since she was tiny. She looks forward to school holidays when she has free time to spend baking for picnics, family celebrations and bake sales.

She won her first cookery competition at the age of five when, along with her sister Lara, she entered her 'funny face pizza' into the local village country show.

Amy has literally taken over the family kitchen, experimenting with cooking and baking and, aged thirteen, set up her own cupcake and cake business, receiving large orders, with celebrities among her clients.

Following requests from friends, family and teachers for baking tips, Amy started to record her recipes. She was featured in the *Sunday Express* newspaper and her first recipes were published in the paper's magazine *S Mag* when she was just fourteen.

Now Amy has selected her most gorgeous recipes and collected them in this stunning book to share with you. You can learn how to make everything from back-to-basic and traditional classics handed down through generations to show-stoppers that will take your breath away.

For this book, Amy has loved being responsible for all aspects of design, style and presentation at every stage. When she is not in the kitchen writing, creating and baking her delicious recipes, Amy likes fine art and performing as a singer and harpist.

Contents

Introduction   11

Spring   13

It is lovely to see the first signs of the warmer weather. Flowers in bloom, and a chance for families to gather together for special occasions such as Mother's Day and Easter.

- Mother's Day   15
- Easter   37

Summer   59

Long, warm months to enjoy picnics with friends and family. A perfect time to organise a cake sale or host a tea party for friends.

- Cake sale (Baking is a great way to help raise funds for charity)   61
- Picnic   85
- Afternoon Tea Party   103
- Father's Day   135

Autumn   141

Delicious autumnal treats to bake and enjoy during this cold season that are sure to warm you up.

- Halloween   143
- Autumn/Bonfire Night   157

Winter   171

It might be getting cold outside, but there is much to look forward to in this chilly season. Winter is about wrapping up warm inside and enjoying lavish bakes, colourful frosting and hearty portions.

- Christmas   173
- New Year   205
- Valentine's Day   209

Conversion Tables   221
Amy's Baking Essentials   222
Directory   225
Index   227
Ackowledgements   232

Introduction

Ever since I was a little girl, I have had a passion for cooking and baking. My mum would always involve my sister Lara and me when entertaining or when baking for special occasions, and we loved to help her with the preparations. Baking is an enjoyable aspect of cooking and I have happy memories of Lara and me baking and decorating biscuits and cakes for all occasions with my mum. Whether you are baking for a birthday celebration, fundraising event, or as a gift for family and friends, it is special because it has been homemade with fresh ingredients, and baked with thought and love.

My mum would tell us stories of how my grandparents would set aside time in their busy lives to spend in the kitchen baking with her and her siblings, each having their own speciality, such as cheese straws or barley sugar.

It was not long before I wanted to experiment on my own in the kitchen. Baking is a chance to forget everyday commitments and is really worth making the time for. Although it is time-consuming, it is fun and relaxing to do and extremely rewarding when your hard work is appreciated and you are making someone happy.

Baking gives me the chance to express my creativity, inspired by my garden, the flowers and the changing seasons.

Writing this, my first book, has been an exciting venture and combines my favourite traditional recipes handed down from my mum and grandparents – such as a classic Victoria sponge and English madeleines – to today's modern trends such as cupcakes and cake pops, beautifully decorated with my own handmade flower and butterfly fondant decorations.

I have created recipes for entertaining family and friends, from my heart-shaped ombre ruffle cake, fondant fancies to serve for an afternoon tea, my own unique red velvet cupcake ice cream, to my gingerbread house made from scratch. All challenging but enjoyable projects and so satisfying when you see the end result.

It is lovely to share something you have made yourself, and all my recipes make a perfect and thoughtful gift – such as a cupcake bouquet for Mother's Day, an Easter bonnet biscuit in its own individual hat box, or a handmade Christmas stocking filled with treats.

I hope you will feel inspired and enjoy following and baking my recipes as much as I do. Once you start baking you won't want to stop!

Amy x

For the tastiest results I would recommend using free-range organic eggs where possible. It is also advisable to make sure the butter, eggs and milk are all at room temperature before you begin to get the best rise out of your bakes. NB All eggs used in my recipes are large, all butter is unsalted and I use whole milk.

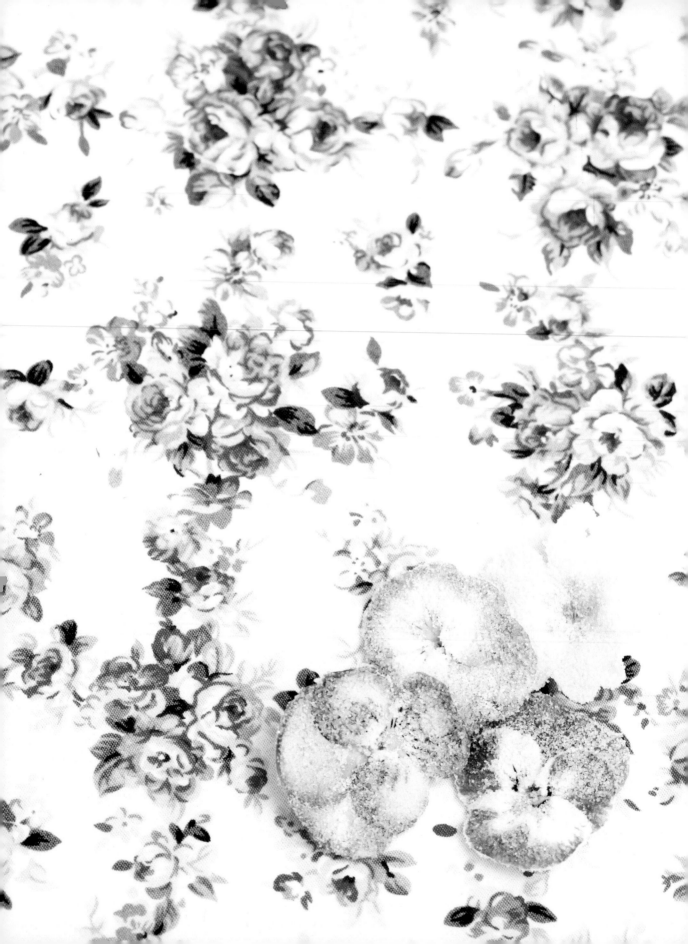

SPRING

Mother's Day

Make your mum feel loved and appreciated by baking some pretty and delicious treats for her on her special day.

Cupcake Bouquet   16

Mother's Day Cupcakes   18

Handmade Fondant Decorations   22

Crystallised Rose Petals and Flowers   24

White Chocolate, Raspberry and Rose Petal Cake   25

French Macarons   29

'As Pretty as a Picture' Mother's Day Biscuits   32

CUPCAKE BOUQUET

Surprise your mum this Mother's Day with a bouquet of cupcakes.

(MAKES 12)

INGREDIENTS

175g (6oz) butter
175g (6oz) caster sugar
175g (6oz) self-raising flour
3 eggs
1 tsp vanilla extract

For the buttercream:
225g (8oz) butter
450g (1lb) icing sugar
2–3 tbsp milk
1 tsp vanilla extract
Pink food colouring (gel/ paste
  is best)

For your cupcake bouquet:
7–12 prepared vanilla cupcakes
  (depending on the size of your
  pot)
Cocktail sticks
Flowerpot
Polystyrene to fit your pot and 1
  inch shorter than the top

Amy's Tip

To avoid your cupcakes spilling over the edge of the cases, only fill them two-thirds full with cake mixture.

METHOD

1. Preheat the oven to 180°C/fan 160°C/350°F/gas mark 4 and line a 12-hole muffin tin with paper cupcake or muffin cases.
2. Put the butter, caster sugar, eggs and vanilla extract into the bowl of a free-standing electric mixer (or you can use a handheld electric whisk and mixing bowl). Sift in the flour and beat for 1–2 minutes until light and creamy. Divide the mixture evenly between the paper cases.
3. Bake in the preheated oven for 20–25 minutes or until well risen and a skewer inserted into one of the cakes comes out clean. Remove from the oven and leave to cool in the tin for 10 minutes. Transfer to a wire rack to cool completely.
4. Meanwhile, prepare the buttercream. Beat the butter until soft and creamy. Sift the icing sugar and add to the creamed butter in two stages alternating with the milk, mixing on a low speed. When fully incorporated add the vanilla extract and beat for 3–5 minutes on a higher speed. Mix in a little pink food colouring using the tip of a cocktail stick until you reach your desired shade.
5. Spoon the pink buttercream into a piping bag fitted with a star nozzle and swirl it on top of the cupcakes, from the centre outwards. Once iced, place your cupcakes in the fridge while you prepare the flowerpot.
6. Place the polystyrene in the flowerpot. Put two cocktail sticks in each area where you want a cupcake. Around the sides, insert the cocktail sticks at a 45° angle, otherwise the cupcakes will fall off. You will need to raise the centre of the pot with scrunched-up tissue paper.
7. Slide a cupcake onto each pair of cocktail sticks, adjusting as needed to cover polystyrene.
8. Fill in any gaps with fresh flowers and tie a pretty ribbon around the pot.

MOTHER'S DAY CUPCAKES

Treat your mum to tea and scrumptious cupcakes adorned with handmade
fondant flowers and butterflies this Mother's Day.

(MAKES 12)

INGREDIENTS

For the cupcakes:
175g (6oz) butter
175g (6oz) caster sugar
175g (6oz) self-raising flour
3 large eggs
1 tsp vanilla extract

For the buttercream:
225g (8oz) butter
450g (1lb) icing sugar
2–3 tbsp milk
1 tsp vanilla extract
Pink food colouring (gel/paste
  is best)

To decorate you will need:
Handmade fondant rose, flower,
  and butterfly decorations (page 22)
Decorative wrappers
White edible glitter (or another
  colour of your choice)

Amy's Tip

For an extra special finishing
touch, sit each cupcake in a
decorative wrapper.

METHOD

1. Preheat the oven to 180°C/fan 160°C/350°F/gas
mark 4 and line a 12-hole muffin tin with paper cupcake
or muffin cases.

2. Put the butter, caster sugar, eggs and vanilla extract
into the bowl of a free-standing mixer (or you can use
a handheld electric whisk and mixing bowl). Then sift
in the flour, lifting the sieve quite high to incorporate
air, and beat for 1–2 minutes until light and creamy.
Be careful not to overmix. Divide the mixture evenly
between the paper cases.

3. Bake in the preheated oven for 20–25 minutes or until
well risen and a skewer inserted into one of the cakes
comes out clean. Remove from the oven and leave to
cool in the tin for 10 minutes. Transfer to a wire rack to
cool completely.

4. Meanwhile, prepare the buttercream. Beat the butter
until soft and creamy. Sift the icing sugar and add to the
creamed butter in two stages alternating with the milk,
mixing on a low speed. When fully incorporated, add
the vanilla extract and beat for 3–5 minutes on a higher
speed.

5. Divide the buttercream between two bowls. Leave
one bowl of buttercream white. Use the tip of a cocktail
stick to add a little pink food colouring to the other bowl
of buttercream.

6. Spoon the white buttercream into a piping bag
fitted with a star nozzle and swirl it on top of six of
the cupcakes. Fill a second piping bag with the pink
buttercream and swirl it on top of the remaining six
cupcakes.

7. Dust with edible glitter and decorate with handmade
fondant roses, flowers and butterflies.

HANDMADE FONDANT DECORATIONS

Make some beautiful handmade fondant decorations to make your Mother's Day cupcakes extra special.

INGREDIENTS

White fondant icing

Pink fondant icing (or you can use food colouring to colour your white fondant icing)

Green fondant icing (or you can use food colouring to colour your white fondant icing)

Icing sugar for dusting

You will need:

A 5cm (2 inch) round cutter

Large butterfly-shaped plunger cutter

Small butterfly-shaped plunger cutter

Leaf plunger cutter

1cm (½ inch) flower plunger cutter

Edible pearls

Pearl dust

Fine decorating brush

Small rolling pin

Sponge

METHOD

1. To make a simple rose, knead pink or white fondant icing until it is pliable. Dust your surface lightly with icing sugar and roll out the icing to a thickness of 3mm (⅛ inch). Cut out two round shapes, place one a quarter of the way onto the other and roll it tightly. Separate the edges to look like petals. Use a decorating brush to apply pearl dust to finish. Leave on some baking parchment for an hour to dry and firm.

2. To make the butterflies, knead pink or white fondant icing until it is pliable. Dust your surface lightly with icing sugar and roll out the icing to a thickness of about 5mm (¼ inch) and cut out using large and small butterfly cutters. Using a decorating brush, finish with pearl dust. Leave for an hour to dry and firm.

3. To make the small flowers, knead pink or white fondant icing until it is pliable. Dust your surface lightly with icing sugar and roll out the fondant icing to a thickness of about 5mm (¼ inch). Use a 1cm (½ inch) flower plunger cutter to cut out little flowers, lifting the cutter away from the fondant with the flower still intact. Place on the top of a clean sponge and press the top of the plunger to remove the flower and form the petals at the same time. Brush with pearl dust and finish by placing an edible pearl in the centre of each flower. Leave on some baking parchment to dry and firm.

4. To make leaves, knead green fondant icing until it is pliable. Dust your surface lightly with icing sugar and roll out the fondant icing to a thickness of 3mm (⅛ inch) and use a leaf plunger cutter to cut out. Leave for an hour to dry and firm.

CRYSTALLISED ROSE PETALS AND FLOWERS

This is the perfect decoration for any cake. It is best to crystallise flowers a few hours before you need them as they will need time to dry.

INGREDIENTS

1 egg white, lightly whisked

75g (3oz) caster sugar

Edible flowers, such as primroses, violas, pansies or rose petals

You will need:

A fine decorating brush

METHOD

1. Collect your flowers, making sure they are pesticide and insect-free. Dip a decorating brush into the egg white and carefully brush the flowers or petals, using just enough egg white to cover the surface. Spoon sugar over each flower or petal, then shake off the excess. Dry the petals on baking parchment for at least 3 hours before using – make them the day before if you can.

2. Store your petals in an airtight box or tin lined with kitchen paper. They will keep for two weeks – any longer and they start to lose their colour.

Amy's Tip

As the weather gets warmer and your garden begins to bloom, why not see what you have growing with which to decorate your bakes, before you buy flowers?

WHITE CHOCOLATE, RASPBERRY AND ROSE PETAL CAKE

Bake this beautiful and delicious cake for your mum to share with her loved ones on her special day.

(SERVES 10–12)

INGREDIENTS

For the cake:

350g (12oz) butter, plus a little
   more for greasing tins
350g (12oz) caster sugar
350g (12oz) self-raising flour
6 eggs
2 tsp vanilla extract
2 tsp rosewater

For the rose syrup:

110g (4oz) caster sugar
60ml (2fl.oz) water
1 tsp rosewater

For the white chocolate and rose
   buttercream filling:
110g (4oz) butter
225g (8oz) icing sugar
150g (5oz) white chocolate
1–2 tbsp milk
1 tbsp rose syrup
1 tsp vanilla extract

For the raspberry glacé icing:
110g (4oz) raspberries
275g (10oz) icing sugar

METHOD

1. Preheat the oven to 180°C/fan 160°C/350°F/gas mark 4. Grease 2 x 20cm (8 inch) cake tins and line the bases with baking parchment. To do this, draw around the base of the cake tins and cut out.

2. Put the butter, caster sugar, eggs, rosewater and vanilla extract into the bowl of a free-standing electric mixer (or you can use a handheld electric whisk and mixing bowl). Then sift in the flour, lifting the sieve quite high to incorporate air, and beat for 1–2 minutes until light and creamy. Divide the mixture between the two cake tins, smoothing the surface of the cake mixture with a spatula or the back of a spoon.

3. Bake for 45 minutes or until well risen and a skewer inserted into the middle of the cakes come out clean. Leave to cool in the tins for 10 minutes. Turn out onto a wire rack, peel off the baking parchment and leave to cool completely.

4. To make the rose syrup, put the sugar in a pan with 60ml (2fl.oz) water and heat until the sugar has dissolved. Turn up the heat and let it bubble for 1–2 minutes, then remove from the heat. Add the rosewater (be careful as the syrup will be very hot). Spoon half the syrup over the cakes and set aside.

5. Melt the white chocolate in a bowl over a pan of gently simmering water, making sure the water is not touching the bottom of the bowl. Stir the mixture every now and then until all of the chocolate has melted.

For the filling:
150g (5oz) raspberries

To decorate:
Crystallised rose petals (page 24)
Crystallised rose fragments

Leave the melted chocolate to cool until needed.

6. Meanwhile, prepare the white chocolate and rose buttercream. Beat the butter until soft and creamy. Sift the icing sugar and gradually add with the milk to the creamed butter mixing on a low speed. When fully incorporated add 2 tbsp of the syrup, the rosewater, the vanilla extract and the cooled chocolate and beat for 3–5 minutes on a higher speed until soft and fluffy.

7. Add 1 tbsp of the syrup to the raspberries and crush them with a fork. Put the raspberries through a sieve into a bowl and discard the seeds. Sift in the icing sugar and mix to a smooth icing.

8. To assemble, place one cake, flat-side up, on a plate or cake stand, and top with the white chocolate and rose buttercream and then arrange the raspberries on top. Sandwich the second cake on top. Pour and smooth the raspberry glacé icing over the top, letting it drizzle down the sides. To decorate, I used my handmade crystallised rose petals (page 24) and crystallised rose fragments.

FRENCH MACARONS

Your mum will be delighted to receive a beautifully wrapped
gift box of French macarons.

(MAKES APPROX. 20)

INGREDIENTS

For the macaron mixture:
175g (6oz) icing sugar
110g (4oz) ground almonds
75g (3oz) caster sugar
3 egg whites
Pinch of salt
Yellow food colouring (gel/paste
  is best)
Pink food colouring (gel/paste
  is best)
Green food colouring (gel/paste
  is best)

For the lemon buttercream filling:
50g (2oz) butter
110g (4oz) icing sugar, sifted
1 tbsp lemon juice
Yellow food colouring (gel/paste
  is best)

For the rose buttercream filling:
50g (2oz) butter
110g (4oz) icing sugar, sifted
1 tbsp milk
Rosewater
Pink food colouring (gel/paste is
  best)

TO MAKE THE MACARONS:

1. Preheat the oven to 150°C/fan 130°C/300°F/gas mark 2. Sift the icing sugar and ground almonds into a bowl to remove any lumps.

2. In a separate bowl, whisk the egg whites with a pinch of salt to soft peaks, then gradually whisk in the caster sugar until thick and glossy.

3. Using a spatula, fold half the almond and icing sugar mixture into the meringue. Add the remaining half then cut and fold the mixture until it is shiny and has a thick, ribbon-like consistency as it falls from the spatula.

4. To make assorted colours as I have, divide the mixture into three small bowls. a. For rose flavour macarons, in one bowl add ¼ tsp rosewater and mix in a little pink food colouring using the tip of a cocktail stick. b. For the white chocolate and pistachio ganache macarons, add a little green food colouring. c. For lemon flavoured macarons add ½ tsp lemon juice and mix in a little yellow food colouring.

5. Line 2–3 baking trays with baking parchment. Pipe 4cm (1½ inch) rounds of the macaron mixture, about 1cm across, onto the baking trays. You can draw around a round cutter onto the baking parchment to make an outline to help you. Give the baking trays a sharp tap on the work surface to make sure they don't go flat in the oven. Leave to stand at room temperature for 30 minutes to form a slight skin. This is important – you should be able to touch them lightly without any mixture sticking to your finger. Bake for 15–20 minutes. Remove from the oven and cool.

6. Meanwhile, make the fillings.

For the white chocolate and
  pistachio ganache filling:
60ml (2fl.oz) double cream
40g (1½oz) white chocolate,
  chopped
10g (½oz) pistachio kernels
1 tbsp caster sugar

Amy's Tip

Alternatively, you could fill your
lemon macarons with my delicious
lemon curd (see recipe p44)

TO MAKE THE LEMON BUTTERCREAM:

1. Cream the butter and icing sugar until combined, incorporating the lemon juice. Add a little yellow food colouring using the tip of a cocktail stick. Mix until soft and creamy.

2. Fill a piping bag fitted with a round 1cm (½ inch) nozzle and pipe the lemon buttercream filling onto half of the yellow macaron shells. Sandwich the other half of the yellow macaron shells on top.

TO MAKE THE ROSE BUTTERCREAM:

1. Cream the butter and icing sugar until combined, incorporating the milk. Add ¼ tsp rosewater and mix in a few drops of pink food colouring using the tip of a cocktail stick. Mix until soft and creamy.

2. Fill a piping bag fitted with a round 1cm (½ inch) nozzle and pipe the rose buttercream filling onto half of the pink macaron shells. Sandwich the other half of pink macaron shells on top.

TO MAKE THE WHITE CHOCOLATE AND PISTACHIO GANACHE FILLING:

1. Heat the cream in a saucepan until it is steaming. Put the white chocolate into a bowl and pour the cream over it. Grind the pistachios and caster sugar in a food processor until fine. Add the ground pistachio and sugar mixture to the white chocolate ganache and mix until combined.

2. Refrigerate for half an hour until cold.

3. When cold remove from the fridge and whisk with an electric whisk to form stiff peaks (take care not to over whisk)

4. Fill a piping bag fitted with a round 1cm (½ inch) nozzle and pipe the filling onto half of the green macaron shells. Sandwich the rest of the green macaron shells on top.

'AS PRETTY AS A PICTURE' MOTHER'S DAY BISCUITS

Bring out your artistic side by hand painting flowers from your garden onto these classic shortbread biscuits for your mother's special day.

(MAKES 10)

INGREDIENTS

For the shortbread biscuits:
225g (8oz) plain flour
150g (5oz) butter, plus a little extra
  for greasing tins
50g (2oz) caster sugar
1 tsp crushed dried or fresh
  lavender

For the glacé icing:
500g (1lb 2oz) icing sugar
5–6 tbsp water
Assorted coloured cake dusts
Assorted food colourings (gel/
  paste is best)

You will need:
A fine decorating brush
A small piping bag
Cocktail sticks

Amy's Tip

When mixing your cake dusts you can use an artist's palette, but if you don't have one, a plate is a good substitute.

METHOD

1. Preheat the oven to 180°C/fan 160°C/350°F/gas mark 4 and lightly grease two baking trays.

2. In the bowl of an electric mixer, mix together the butter and sugar until they are combined. Sift the flour into the mixture, add the lavender and mix on a low speed until the dough comes together. Lightly flour your work surface. Turn the dough out and knead and pat into a flat disc. Wrap in cling film and chill for 30 minutes.

3. On a floured surface, roll out to an even thickness of 5mm (¼ inch) and cut out using a 9cm (3½ inch) round cutter. Use a palette knife to transfer the biscuits to the greased baking trays. Bake in the preheated oven for 10–15 minutes or until they are a pale golden colour. Remove from the oven and cool on a wire rack.

4. To make the glacé icing, gradually mix together the icing sugar and water a tablespoon at a time until you have a runny icing. If it is too thin, add some more icing sugar, and if it is too thick, add some more water. Turn the top half of the piping bag inside out. Place the piping bag into a tall glass or jug and pour in the icing. Make a small snip in the tip of the piping bag, and pipe a steady outline around each biscuit. Snip the tip of the piping bag again to make a slightly larger hole, and pipe and fill in (flood) the centres of the biscuits. Use a cocktail stick to carefully spread and fill in any gaps up to the piped outline, being careful not to let the icing overflow around the edges. When set, mix a little water into the coloured cake dusts and pick a flower from your garden to copy. Using a fine decorating brush, paint a flower onto your biscuit.

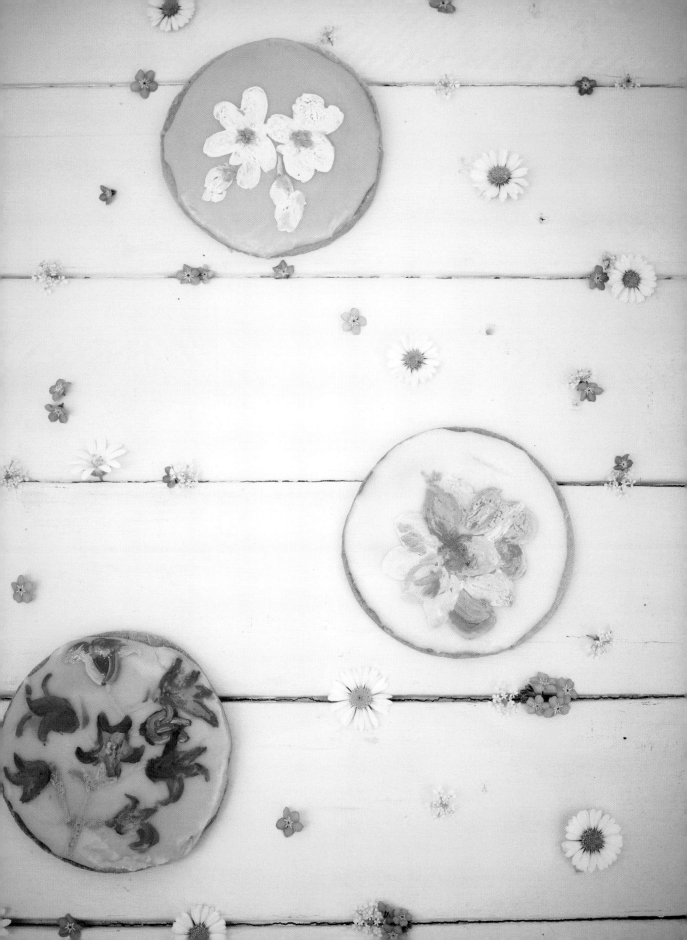

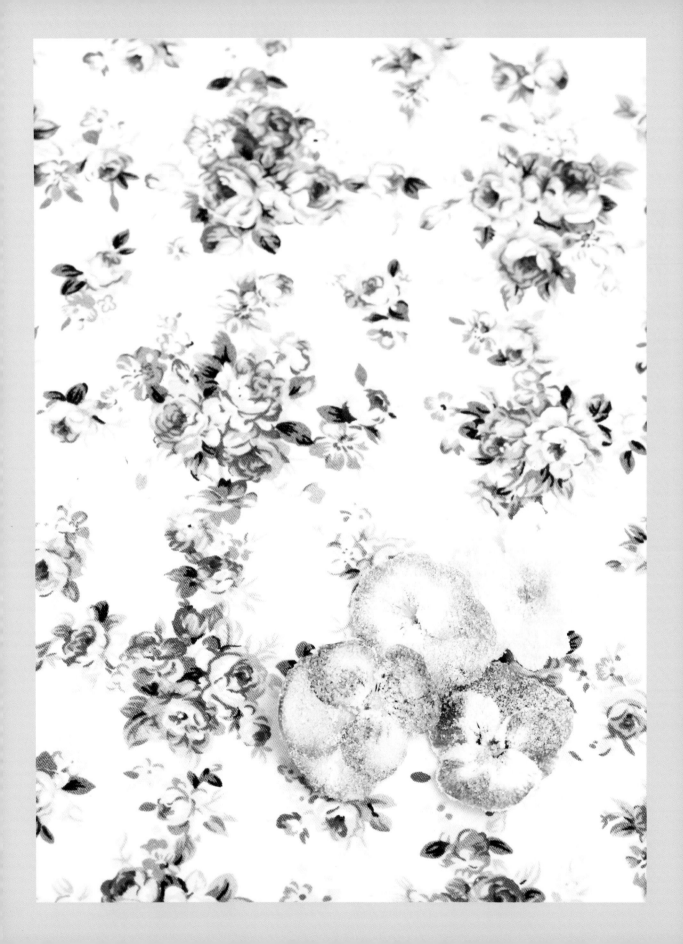

Easter

Perfect spring treats for a family gathering, inspired by the colourful flowers in bloom at this time of year.

Fondant Daffodils   38

Lemon Daffodil Cupcakes   40

Fabergé Easter Egg Biscuits   42

Lemon Curd   44

Lemon Layer Easter Cake   47

Chocolate Easter Nest Cupcakes   48

Easter Bonnet Biscuits   51

Raspberry Iced Bunny Biscuits   54

Pastel Easter Eggs   56

FONDANT DAFFODILS

Yellow fondant icing

Icing sugar for dusting

For the glacé icing – to assemble
  daffodils

110g (4oz) icing sugar

1–2 tsp water

Yellow food colouring (gel/paste
  is best)

You will need:

Small rolling pin

4cm (1½ inch) daffodil cutter –
  or nearest size available

Foam pad

Piping bag

Small ball tool

Number 1.5 icing nozzle

Baking parchment

TO MAKE THE GLACÉ ICING:

1. Sift the icing sugar into a bowl and gradually add the water until you have a smooth icing.

2. Add a little yellow food colouring using the tip of a cocktail stick until you reach your desired shade. Cover bowl with cling film and set aside.

TO MAKE THE DAFFODILS:

1. Dust the work surface lightly with icing sugar. Roll out the fondant icing to the thickness of 3mm (⅛ inch). Cut out two petal layers and one trumpet shape with the daffodil cutter.

2. Place the pieces on the foam pad. Use the small ball tool to thin the petal edges and to thin and frill the longer curved edge of the daffodil trumpet.

3. Lift the daffodil trumpet and roll it up, with the frilled edge facing upwards.

4. Fit the piping bag with the icing nozzle and fill with the prepared yellow glacé icing. Fit the two petal layers together with some icing, ensuring the upper layer sits between the petals on the base layer. Pipe a pearl of icing in the centre of the upper layer.

5. Fix the daffodil trumpet into position in the centre of the daffodil. Repeat until you have enough daffodils. Leave on some baking parchment for 1 hour to dry and firm.

LEMON DAFFODIL CUPCAKES

These zingy lemon cupcakes, topped with delicate handmade daffodils, are a perfect treat for a warm spring day or an Easter tea.

(MAKES 12)

INGREDIENTS

For the lemon curd filling:
1 x jar shop-bought or homemade
  lemon curd (recipe page 44)

For the cupcakes:
175g (6oz) butter
175g (6oz) caster sugar
175g (6oz) self-raising flour
3 eggs
Finely grated zest and the juice of
  1 lemon

For the lemon buttercream:
225g (8oz) butter
450g (1lb) icing sugar
2–3 tbsp lemon juice

To decorate:
12 fondant daffodils (recipe
  page 38)

Amy's Tip

When dividing the mixture into your paper cases, use an ice cream scoop to get a professional finish and evenly sized cakes.

METHOD

1. If using homemade lemon curd, prepare following the recipe on page 44.

2. Preheat oven to 180°C/fan 160°C/350°F/gas mark 4 and line a 12-hole muffin tin with paper cupcake or muffin cases.

3. Put the butter, caster sugar, eggs, lemon zest and lemon juice into the bowl of a free-standing electric mixer (or you can use a handheld electric whisk and mixing bowl). Then sift in the flour, lifting the sieve quite high to incorporate air, and beat for 1–2 minutes until light and creamy. Divide the mixture evenly between the paper cases.

4. Bake in the preheated oven for 20–25 minutes or until well risen and a skewer inserted into one the cakes comes out clean. Remove from the oven and leave to cool in the tin for 10 minutes. Transfer to a wire rack to cool completely.

5. Once the cupcakes are cooled, using an apple corer or cupcake corer, make a hole in the centre of the top of each cupcake, being careful not to push the corer through the bottom of the cake. Spoon the lemon curd into a piping bag and fill the hole in each cupcake.

6. Meanwhile, prepare the lemon buttercream. Beat the butter until soft and fluffy. Sift the icing sugar, and add to the creamed butter in two additions, mixing on a low speed, incorporating the lemon juice, and beat for 3–5 minutes on a higher speed. Spoon the buttercream into a piping bag fitted with a large star nozzle and swirl it on top of the cupcakes.

7. Top each cupcake with a fondant daffodil (page 38).

FABERGÉ EASTER EGG BISCUITS

Hang these beautifully decorated Fabergé Easter egg biscuits from an Easter tree this spring.

(MAKES 10)

INGREDIENTS

For the shortbread biscuits:
225g (8oz) plain flour
150g (5oz) butter, plus a little extra
  for greasing tins
50g (2oz) caster sugar
Finely grated zest of 1 lemon

For the lemon glacé icing:
500g (1lb 2oz) icing sugar
5–6 tbsp lemon juice
Pastel food colourings (gel/paste
  is best)

You will need:
Egg-shaped cutter
Small piping bag
Cocktail sticks
Narrow ribbon

Amy's Tip

You can make an Easter tree, like I have, by gathering some twigs from the garden and placing them in a vase or jug.

METHOD

1. Preheat the oven to 180°C/fan 160°C/350°F/gas mark 4 and lightly grease two baking trays.
2. In a bowl of an electric mixer, mix together the butter, sugar and lemon zest until combined. Sift in the flour and mix on a low speed until the dough comes together. Lightly flour your work surface. Turn the dough out and knead into a flat disc. Wrap in cling film and chill.
3. On a floured surface, roll out the dough to a thickness of 5mm (¼ inch) and cut out using an egg-shaped cutter. Use a straw to make a small hole in the biscuits to thread a ribbon through when baked. Place on the prepared baking trays and bake for 10–15 minutes or until a pale golden colour. Remove from the oven and cool.
4. When they have cooled, make the glacé icing. Mix the lemon juice a tablespoon at a time into the icing sugar until you have a smooth, runny icing. If it is too thin, add some more icing sugar, and if it is too thick, add some more lemon juice or a little water. Divide the icing into separate bowls and add pastel shades of food colouring using the tip of a cocktail stick. Turn the top half of the piping bag inside out. Place the piping bag in a tall glass or jug to pour the icing in. Snip a small hole in the tip of the piping bag and pipe a steady outline around each biscuit. Snip the tip of the piping bag again to make a slightly larger hole, and pipe and fill in (flood) the centres of the biscuits. Use a cocktail stick to carefully fill in any gaps. Decorate with polka dots or fondant flowers (see page 22).
5. When they have set, thread a narrow ribbon through the hole in the biscuit to hang on an Easter tree.

LEMON CURD

I like to keep a jar of my homemade lemon curd in the fridge for using in my recipes.

(MAKES 1 X 340G JAR)

INGREDIENTS

4 unwaxed lemons, zest and juice
200g (7oz) caster sugar
100g (3½oz) butter, cubed
3 eggs, plus 1 egg yolk

Amy's Tip

Lemon curd is a delicious alternative filling for my jam tart recipe.

METHOD

1. Put the lemon zest and juice, the sugar and the butter into a heatproof bowl. Place the bowl over a pan of gently simmering water, making sure the water is not touching the bottom of the bowl. Stir the mixture every now and then until all the butter has melted.

2. Lightly whisk the eggs and egg yolk and stir them into the lemon mixture. Whisk until all of the ingredients are well combined, then leave to cook for 10–15 minutes, stirring every now and again, until the mixture is thick enough to coat the back of a spoon.

3. Remove the lemon curd from the heat and leave to one side to cool, stirring occasionally. Once cooled, strain the lemon curd through a sieve and chill until needed.

LEMON LAYER EASTER CAKE

This mouth-watering lemon cake makes a perfect treat for your loved ones after your Easter Sunday roast lunch.

(SERVES 12)

INGREDIENTS

For the lemon curd:
1 x jar shop-bought or homemade
   lemon curd (recipe page 44)

For the cake:
400g (14oz) butter, plus extra
   for greasing
400g (14oz) caster sugar
400g (14oz) self-raising flour
7 eggs
Zest of 3 lemons
3 tbsp lemon juice

For the lemon buttercream:
225g (8oz) butter
450g (1lb) icing sugar, sifted
2 tbsp lemon juice

Crystallised flowers to decorate
   (see Directory, page 225)

METHOD

1. If using homemade lemon curd, prepare following the recipe on page 44.

2. Preheat the oven to 180°C/fan 160°C/350°F/gas mark 4. Grease 3 x 20cm (8 inch) cake tins and line the bases with baking parchment. To do this draw around the base of the cake tins onto baking parchment and cut out.

3. Put the butter, caster sugar, eggs, lemon juice and lemon zest into the bowl of a free-standing electric mixer (or you can use a handheld electric whisk and mixing bowl). Then sift in the flour, lifting your sieve quite high to incorporate air, and mix until light and creamy.

4. Divide the mixture between the prepared tins and bake for about 50 minutes or until well risen and a skewer inserted into the middle of one of the cakes comes out clean. Remove the cakes from the oven and leave to cool in the tins before turning out onto wire racks. Peel off the baking parchment and leave to cool completely.

5. While the cakes are cooling, make the lemon buttercream by beating the butter until soft and creamy. Add the lemon juice and zest and beat again until smooth. Gradually beat in the icing sugar starting on a low speed. Use two thirds of the buttercream to fill the cake layers and top each layer with lemon curd. Spread the top with the remaining buttercream, and finish with crystallised flowers (page 24).

CHOCOLATE EASTER
NEST CUPCAKES

These vanilla and chocolate Easter nest cupcakes make a great Easter gift for family and friends. They're very popular with children.

(MAKES 12)

INGREDIENTS

For the vanilla cupcakes:
175g (6oz) self-raising flour
175g (6oz) butter
175g (6oz) caster sugar
3 eggs
1 tsp vanilla extract

For the chocolate buttercream:
225g (8oz) butter
400g (14oz) icing sugar
2 tbsp cocoa powder
2–3 tbsp milk

For decorating:
White fondant icing
36 sugar coated mini chocolate eggs
Pink food colouring (gel/paste
 is best)

You will need:
Small bunny-shaped cutter
Small rolling pin

METHOD

1. Preheat the oven to 180°C/fan 160°C/350°F/gas mark 4 and line a 12-hole muffin tin with paper cupcake or muffin cases.

2. Put the butter, caster sugar, eggs and vanilla extract into the bowl of a free-standing electric mixer (or you can use a handheld electric whisk and mixing bowl). Then sift in the flour and beat for 1–2 minutes until light and creamy. Divide the mixture evenly between the paper cases.

3. Bake in the preheated oven for 20–25 minutes or until well risen and a skewer inserted into one the cakes comes out clean. Remove from the oven and leave to cool in the tin for 10 minutes. Transfer to a wire rack to cool completely.

4. Meanwhile, make the chocolate buttercream. Beat the butter until soft and creamy. Sift the icing sugar and cocoa powder, and add to the creamed butter in two additions, mixing on a low speed, incorporating the milk, and beat for 3–5 minutes on a higher speed.

5. Dust your work surface and roll out a small amount of the fondant icing to a thickness of 5mm (¼ inch). Cut out 12 small bunnies using the bunny-shaped cutter. Colour a tiny piece of white fondant icing with a little pink food colouring and using your hands roll 12 tiny bunny tails. Leave to one side to dry.

6. Spoon the chocolate buttercream into a piping bag fitted with a star nozzle, and swirl it on top of the cooled cupcakes. Top with three mini eggs and a fondant bunny to finish.

EASTER BONNET BISCUITS

You can surprise your friends this Easter with beautiful Easter bonnets in their own hat boxes.

(MAKES 10)

INGREDIENTS

For the shortbread biscuits:
225g (8oz) plain flour
150g (5oz) butter, plus extra
 for greasing
50g (2oz) caster sugar

For the glacé icing:
500g (1lb 2oz) icing sugar, sifted
5–6 tbsp water
Pastel coloured food colourings
 (gel/paste is best)

To decorate:
Marshmallows
Seedless jam
Cocktail sticks
Small paintbrush
Ribbon, bows and flowers

Amy's Tip

Buy a small round gift box, line with pretty tissue paper and decorate it with ribbon to look like a hat box.

METHOD

1. Preheat the oven 180°C/fan 160°C/350°F/gas mark 4, and lightly grease 2–3 baking trays.

2. In the bowl of an electric mixer fitted with a paddle attachment, mix the butter and sugar until combined. Sift in the flour and mix on a low speed until a dough forms. Lightly flour your work surface. Turn the dough out and knead and shape into a flat disc. Wrap in cling film and chill for 30 minutes.

3. Roll out to thickness of 5mm (¼ inch) and cut out using a 9cm (3½ inch) wide round cutter. Place onto the prepared baking trays and bake for 10–15 minutes or until a pale golden colour. Remove from the oven then leave to cool on a wire rack.

4. Once the biscuits are cool, gradually mix the water into the icing sugar and beat until smooth and you have a runny icing. Divide the icing between three bowls and add a small amount of assorted food colouring to each.

5. Spread the base of a marshmallow with a little jam and fix to the middle of each biscuit. Turn the top half of the piping bag inside out. Place the piping bag in a tall glass or jug and pour in the icing. Make a small snip in the tip of the piping bag and pipe a steady outline around each biscuit. Snip the tip of the piping bag again to make a slightly larger hole, and pipe and fill in (flood) the centres of the biscuits, covering the marshmallows as well. Use a cocktail stick to carefully spread around the brim and fill in any gaps up to the piped outline, being careful not to let the icing overflow around the edges.

6. Finally, make them look like beautiful bonnets with ribbon, bows and flowers.

RASPBERRY ICED BUNNY BISCUITS

These bunnies have no artificial colours, so they'll be loved by parents as much as their children.

(MAKES APPROX. 15)

INGREDIENTS

For the shortbread biscuits:
110g (4oz) plain flour
60g (2½ oz) butter, plus extra
  for greasing
25g (1oz) caster sugar

For the raspberry glacé icing:
110g (4oz) raspberries
225g (8oz) icing sugar

To decorate you will need:
Bunny-shaped cutter
Small piping bag
Cocktail sticks

Amy's Tip

I often find during mixing that I need to pause to scrape down the dough from the sides of the bowl with a spatula or spoon.

METHOD

1. Preheat the oven to 180°C/fan 160°C/ 350°F/gas mark 4 and lightly grease 2–3 baking trays.

2. In the bowl of an electric mixer fitted with a paddle attachment, mix the butter and sugar until combined. Sift in the flour and mix on a low speed until a dough forms, finishing with your hands if need be. Turn out onto a floured work surface and knead and shape into a flat disc. Wrap in cling film and chill for 30 minutes.

3. Remove from the fridge and roll out to 5mm (¼ inch) thickness on a floured surface, and cut out using a bunny-shaped biscuit cutter (or homemade template).

4. Using a palette knife, transfer the biscuits to the prepared baking trays and bake in the preheated oven for 10 minutes until a pale golden colour.

5. To make the raspberry glacé icing, add 2 tbsp of water to the raspberries and crush them with a fork. Push the raspberries through a sieve into a bowl and discard the seeds. Sift in the icing sugar and mix until smooth and you have a runny, but not too thick icing. Turn the top half of the piping bag inside out. Place the piping bag in a tall glass or jug to pour the icing in. Make a small snip to the tip of the piping bag and pipe a steady outline around each biscuit. Snip the tip of the piping bag again to make a slightly larger hole, and pipe and fill in (flood) the centres of the biscuits. Use a cocktail stick to carefully spread and fill in any gaps up to the piped outline, being careful not to let the icing overflow around the edges.

6. Pipe on a tail with white glacé icing made using a little icing sugar and a few drops of water.

PASTEL EASTER EGGS

Decorate your home this Easter with pastel coloured Easter eggs.

(MAKES 12)

You will need:

Hard-boiled duck eggs

Paper towel or newspaper

Deep bowl or cup

Tongs or large spoon

125ml (4 fl.oz) boiling water

Vinegar

Assorted pastel food
  colourings (gel/paste is best)

METHOD

1. Start with cooled hard-boiled duck eggs.
2. Cover your surface with a sheet of newspaper or paper towels.
3. Fill a container with the mixture of water, vinegar and food colouring.
4. Place each egg on a spoon and dunk into the liquid mixture and leave for 5 minutes until they become the colour you want.
5. Carefully remove each egg and set aside to dry.

SUMMER

CAKE SALE

Victoria Sponge.....£1
per slice

Butterfly Cakes...... 80p

Jam Tarts........... 50p

Coconut Ice........£1

Fudge.............£1

White Choc chip Cookies
£40p

Lemonade..... 75p

Cake Sale

Baking is a great way to help raise funds. These classic family recipes are popular with all ages and are sure to sell out at your cake sale!

Grandma's Victoria Sponge 62

Mint Chocolate Chip Ice Cream 65

Fresh Strawberry Ice Cream 66

My Mum's Butterfly Cakes 69

Homemade Lemonade 72

Strawberry Jam 74

Jam Tarts 76

White Chocolate Chip Cookies 79

Grandad's Coconut Ice 80

Auntie Lynn's Fudge 82

GRANDMA'S VICTORIA SPONGE

This light sponge cake, oozing with homemade jam, is a summer classic. It's great for bake sales, or for a family treat.

(SERVES 8–10)

INGREDIENTS

275g (10oz) butter, plus extra
  for greasing
275g (10oz) caster sugar
275g (10oz) self-raising flour
5 eggs

For the filling:
110g (4oz) butter
225g (8oz) icing sugar, plus extra
  for dusting
1 tbsp milk
1 tsp vanilla extract
Shop-bought or homemade
  strawberry jam (page 74)
Icing sugar for dusting

You will need:
Paper doily

Amy's Tip

To make your Victoria sponge extra special, make your own strawberry jam using the recipe on page 74.

METHOD

1. Preheat the oven to 180°C/fan 160°C/350°F/gas mark 4.
2. Grease two 20cm (8 inch) cake tins and line the bases with baking parchment.
3. Put the butter, caster sugar and eggs into the bowl of a free-standing electric mixer (or you can use a handheld electric whisk and mixing bowl). Then sift in the flour, lifting your sieve quite high to incorporate air, and beat for 1–2 minutes until light and creamy.
4. Divide the mixture evenly between the tins. You can weigh the filled tins if you want to check they are even. Lightly smooth the surface of the cake mixture with a spatula or the back of a spoon.
5. Place the tins on the middle shelf of the oven and bake for about 30 minutes. It is best not to open the door while they are cooking.
6. The cakes are ready when they are golden brown and coming away from the edge of the tins and a skewer inserted into the middle of the cakes comes out clean. Remove them from the oven and leave to cool in their tins for 5 minutes. Carefully turn the cakes on to a wire rack and peel off the baking parchment. Leave to cool completely.
7. To assemble the cake, place one cake upside down onto a plate and spread with plenty of jam.
8. To make the buttercream, beat the butter until soft and creamy. Gradually beat in the icing sugar, milk and vanilla extract. Carefully spread a thick layer of the buttercream on top of the cake spread with jam.
9. Top with the second cake and dust the top with icing sugar using a doily to create a pretty pattern like my grandma showed me when I was little.

MINT CHOCOLATE CHIP ICE CREAM

This fresh mint ice cream will cool you down this summer.

(SERVES 6–8)

INGREDIENTS

250ml (8fl.oz) whole milk

175g (6oz) caster sugar

500ml (16fl.oz) double cream

1 tsp vanilla extract

110g (4oz) mint leaves

75g (3oz) high quality dark
  chocolate (70% cocoa solids)

Green food colouring (gel/paste
  is best)

Amy's Tip

You will need an ice cream maker. The bowl of the ice cream maker will need to be pre-frozen in the freezer for at least 8 hours, or overnight.

METHOD

1. Combine the milk, cream, sugar and vanilla extract in a medium sized saucepan and heat over a medium heat. Stir until the sugar has completely dissolved and the mixture comes to a low boil. Turn the heat to low and simmer for about 4 minutes.

2. Break the mint leaves down a little with a wooden spoon. Add the mint to the saucepan with the milk mixture and cover with a lid. On a low heat, let it steep for 25 minutes.

3. Put a sieve over a large bowl and pour the milk mixture through it to remove the mint leaves. Transfer the bowl into the fridge and chill for 3 hours or overnight. Mix in a little green food colouring using the tip of a cocktail stick until it is a very pale pastel green colour.

4. Process the chilled mixture in an ice cream maker for about 30 minutes or until thickened. Put the container you plan to use for the ice cream in the freezer to chill while the ice cream churns.

5. Chop the chocolate into small chunks and fold the pieces into the churned ice cream. Transfer the ice cream into your chilled container and freeze for at least 4–6 hours before serving. This ice cream remains beautifully easy to scoop even after freezing overnight.

FRESH STRAWBERRY ICE CREAM

This fresh, creamy ice cream is naturally flavoured and coloured. It is a favourite of mine and I hope it will soon be a favourite of yours!

(SERVES 4–6)

INGREDIENTS

275g (10oz) strawberries
50g (2oz) caster sugar
150ml (5floz/¼ pint) double cream
Juice of ½ lemon

METHOD

1. Blend the chopped strawberries in a blender until smooth, then add the remaining ingredients and stir.
2. Churn in an ice cream maker for about 30 minutes until thick and then freeze.

Amy's Tip

You will need an ice cream maker and the ingredients can be doubled. The bowl of the ice cream maker will need to be pre-frozen in the freezer for at least 8 hours or overnight.

MY MUM'S BUTTERFLY CAKES

These easy butterfly cakes were a favourite birthday tradition for our family when we were little, and are perfect to sell at a summer fete or cake sale.

(MAKES 12)

INGREDIENTS

For the cakes:
175g (6oz) butter
175g (6oz) caster sugar
175g (6oz) self-raising flour
3 eggs
1 tsp vanilla extract

For the buttercream:
175g (6oz) butter
350g (12oz) icing sugar, plus extra
  for dusting
2–3 tbsp milk
1 tsp vanilla extract

METHOD

1. Preheat the oven to 180°C/fan 160°C/350°F/gas mark 4 and line a 12-hole muffin tin with paper cupcake or muffin cases.

2. Put the butter, caster sugar, eggs and vanilla extract into the bowl of a free-standing electric mixer (or you can use a handheld electric whisk and mixing bowl). Then sift in the flour, lifting the sieve quite high to incorporate air, and beat for 1–2 minutes until light and creamy. Divide the mixture evenly between the paper cases.

3. Bake in the preheated oven for 20–25 minutes or until well risen and a skewer inserted into one of the cakes comes out clean. Remove from the oven and leave to cool in the tin for 10 minutes. Transfer to a wire rack to cool completely.

4. Meanwhile, prepare the buttercream. Beat the butter until soft and creamy. Sift the icing sugar, and add to the creamed butter in two stages, mixing on a low speed. When fully incorporated add the milk and vanilla extract and beat for 3–5 minutes on a higher speed.

5. Using a small, sharp knife cut out the centre of each cake and slice each scooped-out piece in half.

6. Spread the buttercream into the hollow with a small rounded knife.

7. Reposition the cut out centres on each cake so they resemble butterfly wings.

Amy's Tip
I like to dust each butterfly cake with a little icing sugar to finish.

HOMEMADE LEMONADE

Be refreshed this summer with cool, fresh lemonade – perfect for
hot summer days.

INGREDIENTS
175g (6oz) sugar
250ml (8fl.oz) water
250ml (8fl.oz) lemon juice or
 juice of 4–6 lemons
Around 750ml (1¼ pints) cold
 water (to dilute)

METHOD
1. Make a simple syrup by heating the sugar and 250ml
(8 fl.oz) water in a small saucepan until the sugar is
dissolved completely.
2. While the sugar is dissolving, extract the juice from
4–6 lemons.
3. Pour the juice and the sugar water into a jug. Add
cold water to dilute. Refrigerate for 30–40 minutes. If the
lemonade is a little sweet for your taste, add a little more
lemon juice to it.
4. Serve with ice and sliced lemons.

STRAWBERRY JAM

Make your jam tarts and other bakes even more special by making some fresh strawberry jam to fill them with.

(MAKES 4 x 340G JARS)

INGREDIENTS

1kg (2lbs 2oz) strawberries
1kg (2lbs 2oz) granulated sugar
Juice of 1 lemon

You will need:
4 x 340g jars
Jam funnel

Amy's Tip

Why not try growing your own strawberries in strawberry pots like I do?

METHOD

1. Sterilise the jars. First wash the jars in soapy water and rinse in clear water. Place the jars upturned on a baking tray in the oven preheated to 180°C/fan 160°C/350°F/gas mark 4 for 5 minutes until dry (or you can carefully swill the washed jars with boiled water).

2. Prepare strawberries by washing them and removing tops and greenery. Cut into chunks.

3. Put the strawberries and lemon juice into a large, heavy based saucepan and, on a low heat, simmer gently for an hour.

4. Add the sugar and turn up the heat until the jam temperature rises to setting point.

5. Once the jam has thickened and reached setting point, skim any scum off the top. Test by placing a tea spoon of jam on a chilled saucer. If the surface of the jam wrinkles when pushed it is ready, if not continue to simmer and test again.

6. Leave the jam to cool for 15–20 minutes. Use a jam funnel to ladle into the sterilised jars. Seal with a lid immediately. Label and store in a cool place.

JAM TARTS

These yummy jam tarts are always popular at a summer fete. I like to use equal quantities of butter and lard for a richer and crumblier pastry.

(MAKES 20)

INGREDIENTS

50g (2oz) butter, cubed

50g (2oz) lard or vegetable
  shortening, cubed

225g (8oz) plain flour

1 egg, beaten

Seedless strawberry jam
  (or see my homemade jam
  recipe, page 74)

Amy's Tip

For something more special,
you can top each cooled
jam tart with a swirl of whipped
cream and some halved
strawberries.

METHOD

1. Preheat the oven to 180°C/fan 160°C/350°F/gas mark 4.

2. To make the pastry, sift the flour into a bowl, and using the tips of your fingers rub in the butter and lard, lifting your hands well above the bowl to incorporate as much air as possible, until the mixture resembles breadcrumbs (you can do this by hand or with an electric mixer or food processor). Add the beaten egg and mix with a knife until a dough forms. Then use your hands to bring it together. Knead lightly on a floured surface into a flat disc, then wrap in cling film and chill for 30 minutes.

3. Lightly flour your work surface. Roll out thinly with a floured rolling pin and, using a fluted pastry cutter just a little bigger than the holes of two lightly greased 12-hole tart tins, cut out rounds of pastry and gently push them into the holes so they come up the sides. Any leftover pastry can be gently pushed back into a ball and rolled out to make a few more tarts. Put one heaped teaspoon of jam into each tart. Be careful not to put too much in.

4. Put the trays on the middle shelf of the oven and cook for 15–20 minutes, or until the pastry is golden and the filling is thick and bubbling. Remove from the oven, leave in the tray to firm slightly (be careful as the jam is very hot) then transfer to a wire rack and leave to cool for a few more minutes before serving.

WHITE CHOCOLATE CHIP COOKIES

These melt-in-your-mouth cookies will be loved by all this summer.

(MAKES 24)

INGREDIENTS

110g (4oz) butter, plus extra
  for greasing
110g (4oz) soft light brown sugar
110g (4oz) caster sugar
½ tsp vanilla extract
1 egg, lightly beaten
275g (10oz) self-raising flour
110g (4oz) white chocolate
  chopped into chunks
50g (2oz) salted macadamia nuts,
  roughly chopped

Amy's Tip

If you don't have a bar of white chocolate, you can use white chocolate chips. You can also replace white chocolate with milk chocolate.

METHOD

1. Preheat the oven to 180°C/fan 160°C/350°F/gas mark 4 and lightly grease 2–3 baking trays.

2. Place the butter, sugar and vanilla extract into the bowl of a free-standing electric mixer (or you can use a handheld electric whisk and mixing bowl) and beat together until light and fluffy. Gradually add the egg, beating well after each addition. Sift the flour into the creamed mixture and mix well. Stir in the chocolate chunks along with the chopped nuts.

3. Shape tablespoonfuls of the mixture into small balls and place on the baking trays, putting no more than 6 on each sheet because the cookies will spread during cooking. Bake in the preheated oven for 10–12 minutes, or until just set. Leave to cool on the baking trays for 5 minutes. Transfer the cookies to wire racks to cool completely.

GRANDAD'S COCONUT ICE

I was inspired to make this family favourite after hearing about my grandad's sweet creations.

(MAKES APPROX. 20–30 SQUARES)

INGREDIENTS

250g (9oz) sweetened
  condensed milk
250g (9oz) icing sugar, sifted,
  plus extra for dusting
200g (7oz) desiccated coconut
Pink food colouring (gel/paste
  is best)

Amy's Tip

These sweet treats are
ideal to sell at a cake sale
or summer fete, or to take as
a gift when visiting friends.

METHOD

1. Using a wooden spoon, mix together the condensed milk and icing sugar in a large bowl. It will get very stiff. Work the coconut into the mix until it is well combined – use your hands if you like.

2. Split the mix into two and add a very small amount of food colouring into one half using the tip of a cocktail stick. Knead well to incorporate the colour. Dust a board with icing sugar then shape each half into a smooth rectangle and place one on top of the other. Roll with a rolling pin, re-shaping with your hands every couple of rolls, until you have a rectangle of two-tone coconut ice about 3cm/1¼ inch thick.

3. Transfer to a plate or a board and leave uncovered for at least 3 hours or ideally overnight to set. Cut into squares with a sharp knife. Divide the coconut ice squares into cellophane bags. Tie with a pretty ribbon.

AUNTIE LYNN'S FUDGE

My Auntie Lynn taught me how to make the best ever fudge when I was younger using her special recipe – a favourite in our family.

INGREDIENTS

397g tin condensed milk
150ml (5fl.oz/¼ pint) milk
450g (1lb) demerara sugar
110g (4oz) butter

> **Amy's Tip**
> Try adding some chopped nuts, sea salt, glacé cherries or chocolate chips at the end of step 4.

METHOD

1. Line a 20cm (8 inch) square shallow cake tin with baking parchment.
2. Place the ingredients into a large non-stick saucepan and melt over a low heat, stirring until the sugar dissolves. It may take a while, but if not fully dissolved it will result in a grainy texture.
3. Bring to the boil then simmer for 10–15 minutes, stirring continuously and scraping the base of the pan. Take care while the mixture boils during stirring as the fudge will be very hot. To test it is ready drop a little of the mixture into a jug of ice-cold water. A soft ball of fudge should form. Or check with a sugar thermometer if you have one (approx. 118°C).
4. Remove from the heat and beat the fudge until very thick and starting to set (about 10 minutes).
5. Pour into the prepared tin and leave to cool before cutting into squares.

CAKE SALE

Victoria Sponge.....£1
per slice

Butterfly Cakes...... 80p

Jam Tarts............ 50p

Coconut Ice......... £1

Fudge............... £1

White Choc Chip Cookies
£40p

Lemonade...... 75p

Picnic

This summer, make the most of the warm weather by hosting a picnic for your friends in your garden or the local park.

Bread   86

Blackberry Jam   88

Blackberry Cordial   91

Blackberry Drizzle Muffins   93

Blackberry Cheesecake Jars   94

Cheese Scones   97

Strawberry Basket Cakes   98

Sausage and Caramelised Onion Plaits   101

BREAD

Impress your friends at your picnic by making homemade
bread for your sandwiches.

(MAKES 2 LOAVES)

INGREDIENTS

2lb (900g) strong white bread flour
10g (½oz) powdered dried yeast
20g (¾oz) salt
600ml (20 fl.oz/1 pint) warm water
Olive oil or sunflower oil

2 loaf tins 13 x 23cm (5 x 9 inch)

Amy's Tip

I used smoked salmon, cream
cheese and sliced cucumber
for my sandwiches, but cheese,
ham or egg and cress are other
picnic favourites.

METHOD

1. Combine the flour, yeast, and salt in a large mixing
bowl. Add the water and mix to a rough dough with
your hands. Turn the dough out onto a lightly oiled work
surface and wash your hands.

2. Use your hands to knead the dough: push the dough
out in one direction with the heel of your hand, then
fold it back on itself. Turn the dough 90° and repeat
this process for about 10 minutes until it is smooth and
satiny.

3. Shape the dough into a round. Oil the surface of the
dough and put it in a clean mixing bowl. Cover with
cling film and leave to rise until doubled in size. This will
take about 45 minutes.

4. When risen, turn the dough out onto your work
surface and press all over with your fingertips to deflate
it. Shape into a round and leave to rise again. Heat the
oven to 240°C/fan 220°C/475°F/gas mark 9.

5. Divide your dough into two halves and dust your loaf
tins with flour. With your dough smooth side down, prod
it with your fingertips until it is as wide as your tin is
long. Roll up the dough tightly towards you then press
along the seam with your fingers and lay seam-down.
Stretch the ends and tuck them underneath. Lift up each
loaf and drop it into a tin.

6. Put your loaves into the oven and bake for about 20
minutes. After 10 minutes, turn the heat down to 200°C
fan 180°C/400°F/gas mark 6. Bake until browned and
crusty. When ready, the loaves will feel hollow when you
tap the bottom.

7. Leave to cool completely on a wire rack before slicing.

8. For your picnic, fill your sandwiches with a filling of
your choice.

BLACKBERRY JAM

This sweet blackberry jam is delicious spread on toast.

(MAKES 4 x 340G JARS)

INGREDIENTS

1kg (2lbs 2oz) blackberries
75ml (3 fl.oz) water
1kg (2lbs 2oz) granulated
  white sugar

Amy's Tip

Rather than buying your blackberries, why not pick them? They grow in hedgerows across the country, so keep your eyes peeled!

METHOD

1. Sterilise the jam jars. First wash the jars in soapy water and rinse. Place the jars upturned on a baking tray in the oven preheated to 180°C/fan 160°C/350°F/gas mark 4 for 5 minutes until dry (or you can carefully swill the washed jars with boiled water).

2. Wash the blackberries. Using a large heavy-based bottom saucepan, simmer the blackberries with the water until they are soft.

3. Remove from the heat and stir in the sugar until it has dissolved. Bring to the boil and allow to boil until setting point is reached and the jam has thickened. Test by placing a teaspoon of jam on a chilled saucer. If the surface of the jam wrinkles when pushed it is ready, if not, continue to simmer and test again.

4. Leave the jam to cool. Using a jam funnel, ladle into sterilised jars and seal with a lid immediately. Store in a cool place.

Blackberry jam

BLACKBERRY CORDIAL

This sweet, summery drink will be a hit at your picnic.

INGREDIENTS

1kg (2lbs 2oz) blackberries
200g (7oz) granulated white sugar
Zest of ½ lemon
Lemonade or water, to dilute

METHOD
1. Put the washed blackberries into a saucepan. Heat them slowly until the juice is oozing. Strain through a sieve to remove the pips. Return the juice to the pan and add the sugar and lemon zest and boil for 30 minutes.
2. Pour into sterilised bottles and seal. To serve, add lemonade or water to the cordial.

BLACKBERRY DRIZZLE MUFFINS

These muffins are perfect for a summer picnic.

(MAKES 12)

INGREDIENTS

For the muffins:
250g (9oz) self-raising flour
1 tsp baking powder
50g (2oz) butter
50g (2oz) caster sugar
175g (6oz) blackberries, washed
  and lightly crushed with a fork
Juice and zest of 1 lemon
2 eggs
150ml (5 fl.oz/¼pint) milk

For the blackberry buttercream:
225g (8oz) butter
450g (1lb) icing sugar, sifted
½ punnet blackberries
1 tsp vanilla extract

METHOD

1. Preheat the oven to 200°C/fan 180°C/400°F/gas mark 6 and line a 12-hole muffin tin with paper cupcake or muffin cases.

2. Sift together the flour and baking powder into a large mixing bowl. Using the tips of your fingers rub in the butter. Add the sugar and stir in the washed and crushed blackberries, lemon juice and lemon zest. Gently mix with a spoon. In a separate bowl beat the eggs and the milk together with a whisk then add to the flour mix. Quickly stir together with a fork until incorporated.

3. Divide the mixture into the paper cases until three quarters full and bake for 20–25 minutes. Remove from the oven and leave to cool in the tin for 10 minutes. Transfer to a wire rack to cool completely.

4. Meanwhile, make the blackberry buttercream. Beat the butter until soft and creamy. On a low speed, gradually add the icing sugar in two stages, beating well between each addition. Add the vanilla extract and beat again.

5. Purée the blackberries in a food processor or blender, then push through a sieve to remove the seeds. Discard the seeds and pour into the buttercream. Beat on a low speed until incorporated. Save some to drizzle on your muffins. Now turn up the speed and beat for about 3 minutes until smooth and creamy.

6. Spoon the icing into a piping bag fitted with a star nozzle and swirl onto the muffins. Drizzle with some of the blackberry purée and top with fresh blackberries.

BLACKBERRY CHEESECAKE JARS

These delicious, easy to make and portable cheesecake jars are a perfect addition to your picnic hamper this summer.

(MAKES 5)

INGREDIENTS

110g (4oz) finely ground
  digestive biscuits
225g (8oz) cream cheese
25g (1oz) butter
110g (4oz) caster sugar
3 eggs
125ml (4fl.oz) sour cream
1 tbsp lemon juice
Pinch of salt
110g (4oz) blackberry jam (shop-
bought or recipe page 88)

You will need:
5 small jam jars

METHOD

1. Preheat the oven to 170°C/fan 150°C/325°F/gas mark 3.

2. Beat the cream cheese in a bowl of a free-standing electric mixer (or you can use a handheld electric whisk and mixing bowl) until smooth. Add the sugar and continue to beat for another 3 minutes. Reduce the speed to low and add the eggs, one at a time, beating well after each addition. Increase the speed to medium and add the sour cream, a pinch of salt and the lemon juice. Beat for 3 minutes. Divide the mixture among 5 small jam jars, filling each two-thirds full. Transfer the jars to a deep baking dish and pour in boiling water until it reaches halfway up the sides of the jars. Cover the dish with foil and cut slits into it. Bake for about 35 minutes or until the cheesecakes are set in the centre. Leave to cool, then chill overnight to set.

3. Once set, make the topping. Finely grind the digestive biscuits with a food processor or by hand. Melt the butter and stir it into the biscuit until combined. Line a baking sheet with baking parchment. Bake the topping mixture for 10 minutes and leave to cool.

4. Top each cheesecake with 2 tablespoons of blackberry jam (page 88) and divide the toasted biscuit topping between the jars.

CHEESE SCONES

Spread with chive butter, these mouth-watering cheese scones will be enjoyed at your picnic.

(MAKES 6)

INGREDIENTS

For the chive butter:
450g (1lb) butter
110g (4oz) finely chopped
  fresh chives

For the cheese scones:
50g (2oz) butter, cubed, plus extra
  for greasing
225g (8oz) self-raising flour
1 tsp baking powder
Pinch of salt
100ml (3 fl.oz) milk
110g (4oz) cheddar cheese, grated
1 tsp mustard powder

For the egg wash:
1 egg
Few drops of milk

Amy's Tip

As an alternative to an egg wash glossy top, you could dust with flour using a flour shaker for a soft crust.

TO MAKE THE CHIVE BUTTER:
1. Mash the butter in a large bowl.
2. Add the chopped chives and continue mashing the butter until fully mixed.
3. Spread out a large (30cm/12 inch) square of cling film across your work surface, then scoop the mixed butter onto the plastic. Roll the butter into a cylinder inside the cling film.
4. Tie the excess cling film at the end of the cylinder into a knot or just use little pieces of string to tie off the ends. Chill until needed.

TO MAKE THE CHEESE SCONES:
1. Preheat the oven to 220°C/fan 200°C/425°F/gas mark 7 and lightly grease a baking tray.
2. Sift the flour and baking powder into a mixing bowl. Rub in the butter using the tips of your fingers, lifting your hands well above the bowl to incorporate as much air as possible. Stir in the salt, grated cheese and the mustard powder. Make a well in the centre and pour in the milk. Using a knife, mix to a soft spongy dough. Turn onto a well-floured board and quickly knead out any cracks.
3. Pat out dough and, using a floured rolling pin, roll lightly until 3cm (1¼ inch) thick. Using a floured scone cutter 6cm (2½ inches) wide, stamp out into rounds with a sharp tap taking care not to twist the cutter. Put onto the prepared baking tray and glaze the top with egg wash (lightly whisk the egg with a few drops of milk).
4. Bake near the top of the oven for around 15 minutes until the scones are well risen and golden brown. Remove from the oven and cool on a wire rack. To serve, slice in half and spread with the chive butter.

STRAWBERRY BASKET CAKES

Make these pretty cakes topped with a handmade fondant strawberry this summer.

INGREDIENTS
For the cakes:
175g (6oz) butter
175g (6oz) caster sugar
175g (6oz) self-raising flour
3 eggs
1 tsp vanilla extract

For decorating:
White fondant icing
Red fondant icing
Green fondant icing
Seedless strawberry jam
A basket weave rolling pin
 (see Directory page 225)
A round cutter
A small star-shaped cutter

METHOD
1. Dust the work surface with icing sugar and roll out the white fondant icing to a thickness of 5mm (¼ inch) using the basket weave rolling pin. Cut out 12 round discs to fit the cakes. Set aside for at least 4 hours to allow to dry.

2. To make the fondant strawberries, make around 30 red pea-size balls, and roll on a work surface lightly dusted with icing sugar, elongating them to resemble a strawberry. Using a cocktail stick, poke indentations all over the strawberries. Roll out some green fondant icing ⅛ inch thick on a work surface lightly dusted with icing sugar and cut out 30 tiny leaves with a small star-shaped cutter. Attach a leaf to the top of each strawberry poking in the centres with a taper-cone modelling tool or a cocktail stick and draping the leaf points down the side of the strawberries. Set aside to dry.

3. Preheat the oven to 180°C/fan 160°C/350°F/gas mark 4 and line a 12-hole muffin tin with gingham and/or red paper cupcake or muffin cases.

4. Put the butter, caster sugar, eggs and vanilla extract into the bowl of a free-standing electric mixer (or you can use a handheld electric whisk and mixing bowl). Then sift in the flour, lifting your sieve quite high to incorporate air, and beat for 1–2 minutes until light and creamy. Divide the mixture evenly among the paper cases.

5. Bake in the preheated oven for 20–25 minutes or until risen and a skewer inserted into one of the cakes comes out clean. Remove from the oven and leave to cool in the tin for 10 minutes. Transfer to a wire rack to cool completely.

6. Spread each cake with a thin layer of seedless strawberry jam and place each fondant disc onto a cake.

7. Top each cake with 1–3 fondant strawberries.

SAUSAGE AND CARAMELISED ONION PLAITS

A sophisticated take on sausage rolls.

(MAKES 6)

INGREDIENTS

225g (8oz) plain flour
Pinch of salt
50g (2oz) butter, cubed
50g (2oz) lard or vegetable
  shortening, cubed
1 egg, beaten

For the egg wash:
1 egg
Few drops of milk

For the filling:
350g (12oz) good quality pork
  sausage meat or good quality
  pork sausages with the skins
  removed
1 garlic clove, crushed
1 tsp of fresh sage, chopped
  (or ½ tsp dried sage)
Pinch of salt
1 tsp pepper
2 onions, chopped
2 tbsp olive oil
1 tbsp sugar

1. To make the caramelised onion, heat the olive oil in the pan and add the chopped onion. Cook until softened and golden in colour. Add the sugar, stirring until the onions caramelise. Leave to cool. Preheat the oven to 220°C/fan 200°C/425°F/gas mark 7.

2. To make the pastry, sift the flour and salt into a bowl, and using the tips of your fingers rub in the butter and lard until the mixture resembles fine breadcrumbs. Add the beaten egg and continue to mix using a knife until a dough forms, finishing with your hands. Knead lightly, then wrap in cling film and chill for 30 minutes.

3. To make the filling, combine the sausage meat, garlic, sage, salt and pepper until evenly mixed.

4. Roll out the pastry on a lightly floured work surface to 30cm (12 inch) square. Carefully slice and divide into 3x10cm (4 inch) strips. Slice each strip in half horizontally. Spread a layer of caramelized onion along the centre of each strip of pastry. Place the sausage meat mixture in blocks evenly down the centres, leaving a short 1cm (½ inch) margin at the top and base. Make cuts at an angle at 1cm (½ inch) intervals down both sides of each pastry strip.

5. Fold the top and bottom ends up over the filling and then cover the filling with alternate strips of pastry, first from one side and then the other, to make a plait.

6. Transfer the finished sausage plaits to a lightly greased baking tray and glaze the tops with egg wash.

7. Bake in the preheated oven for 15–20 minutes, then reduce the temperature to 180°C/fan 160°C/350°F/gas mark 4 and bake for another 10–15 minutes until golden brown. Leave to cool, then wrap in foil and chill.

Afternoon Tea Party

Preparing and hosting an afternoon tea party for my friends and family is one of my favourite things to do. You can make it even more special by starting a collection of tea cups and china to use on special occasions.

Two-Tiered Celebration Cake	104
Rose Petal Jam	107
Rosy Teacup Cupcakes	108
How to Make Fondant Roses	110
Raspberry Iced Tea	112
Fresh Floral Ice Cubes	114
Mini Raspberry, Lemon and Chocolate Éclairs	115
Fondant Fancies	118
English Madeleines	120
Cake Pops	123
Mini Strawberries and Cream Cupcakes	124
High Tea Biscuits	126
Mini Pavlovas	128
Scones	131
Birthday Cupcakes	132

TWO-TIERED CELEBRATION CAKE

This beautiful and impressive cake is perfect for a birthday party or a summer tea party.

(SERVES 24)

INGREDIENTS

For the 6-inch cake:

175g (6oz) butter, plus extra
  for greasing
175g (6oz) caster sugar
3 eggs
1 tsp vanilla extract
175g (6oz) self-raising flour

For the 8-inch cake:

350g (12oz) butter, plus extra
  for greasing
350g (12oz) caster sugar
6 eggs
2 tsp vanilla extract
350g (12oz) self-raising flour

For the pink buttercream:

450g (1lb) butter
900g (2lb) icing sugar
2 tbsp milk
2 tsps vanilla extract
Pink food colouring (gel/paste
  is best)

TO MAKE THE CAKES:

1. Preheat the oven to 180°C/fan 160°C/350°F/gas mark 4. Grease a 6-inch (15cm) and an 8-inch (20cm) cake tin. Line the bases with baking parchment. To do this draw around the base of your tins and cut out.

2. To make the 6-inch cake, put the butter, caster sugar, eggs and vanilla extract into the bowl of a free-standing electric mixer (or you can use a handheld electric whisk and mixing bowl). Then sift in the flour, lifting your sieve quite high to incorporate air, and beat until light and creamy.

3. Pour the mixture into the prepared tin and smooth with a palette knife or the back of the spoon.

4. While baking, prepare the mixture for the 8-inch cake using the same method.

5. Bake in the oven until well risen and a skewer inserted into the middle of the cake comes out clean. The 6-inch cake should take around 50 minutes, the 8-inch around 60 minutes.

6. Allow to cool in the tin for 5 minutes before turning out onto a wire rack. Peel off the baking parchment and leave to cool completely.

TO DECORATE:

1. To make the pink buttercream, place the butter in the bowl of a free-standing electric mixer (or you can use a handheld electric whisk and mixing bowl) and beat until soft and creamy.

2. Add the vanilla extract, and gradually add the icing sugar, sifting as you go, and the milk, until light and creamy.

For the white buttercream:
450g (1lb) butter
900g (2lb) icing sugar
2 tbsp milk
2 tsp vanilla extract

You will need:
1 x 15cm (6-inch) cake tin
1 x 20cm (8-inch) cake tin
3 x hollow plastic dowels
  (to support the weight of the top)
1 x 15cm (6-inch) thin cake board
1 x 25.5cm (10-inch) cake board

3. Mix in a little pink colouring using the tip of a cocktail stick until you reach your desired shade.

4. Make the white buttercream the same way as above. Cover with cling film and leave until needed.

5. Using a serrated knife, carefully level and slice each cake into three layers. Sandwich the layers together with some of the white buttercream.

6. Place the larger cake onto a 25.5cm (10-inch) cake board. Place the smaller cake onto a thinner 15cm (6-inch) cake board.

7. Using a palette knife, spread pink buttercream onto each cake evenly and thinly.

8. Using a serrated knife, score and snap the dowels to the depth of the bottom tier, and evenly space and insert the dowels into the centre of the bottom tier.

9. Place the top tier and board on top of the bottom tier.

10. Spoon the remaining pink buttercream into a piping bag fitted with a large round nozzle, and carefully pipe vertical lines around both cakes.

11. Spoon the remaining white buttercream into a piping bag fitted with a star nozzle, and pipe a shell border around the tops and bottoms of the cake.

12. To finish, fill a pretty teacup with fresh flowers, sit it on top of the tiered cake and place your cake onto a cake stand or plate.

ROSE PETAL JAM

Fill your rosy teacup cakes with my fragrant rose petal jam. A wonderful surprise when your guests cut into their cupcakes.

(MAKES 2 JARS)

INGREDIENTS
110g (4oz) scented rose petals
450g (1lb) granulated sugar
1 litre (1¾ pints) water
Juice of 2 lemons

You will need:
2 x 340g (12oz) jars
Jam funnel

Amy's Tip
Look in your garden for scented roses.

METHOD
1. Sterilise the jam jars. First wash the jars in soapy water and then rinse. Place the jars upside down on a baking tray in the oven preheated to 180°C/fan 160°C/350°F/gas mark 4 for 5 minutes until dry (or you can carefully swill the washed jars with boiled water).
2. Pick the petals making sure they are pesticide and insect-free. If the petals are large, tear them into smaller pieces.
3. Put the rinsed and dried petals in a large bowl with half of the sugar. Gently stir together, then cover and leave in a warm place overnight.
4. Add the rest of the sugar, the water and lemon juice to a large pan. On a low heat, stir until the sugar has dissolved, then stir in the rose petal and sugar mix.
5. Simmer for about 20 minutes, then turn up the heat and boil for another 5 minutes, until it thickens and reaches setting point.
6. Leave to cool before using.
7. Ladle any extra jam into the sterilised jars using a jam funnel. Seal with a lid immediately. Store in a cool place.

ROSY TEACUP CUPCAKES

Make your cupcakes extra special at your tea party by serving them in teacups.

(MAKES 12)

INGREDIENTS

For the cupcakes:
175g (6oz) butter
175g (6oz) caster sugar
175g (6oz) self-raising flour
3 eggs
1 tsp vanilla extract

For the buttercream:
225g (8oz) butter
450g (1lb) icing sugar
1 tsp vanilla extract
2–3 tbsp milk
Pink food colouring (gel/paste
  is best)

For decorating:
Rose petal jam (page 107)
White edible glitter (or a colour
  of your choice)
Handmade fondant roses and
  leaves (pages 22 and 110)

Amy's Tip

When dusting cupcakes I use a teaspoon. You can use your fingers, but you may get covered head to toe in glitter.

TO MAKE THE CAKES:

1. Prepare the rose petal jam (page 107)
2. Preheat the oven to 180°C/fan 160°C/350°F/gas mark 4 and line a 12-hole muffin tin with paper cupcake or muffin cases.
3. Put the butter, caster sugar, eggs and vanilla extract into the bowl of a free-standing electric mixer. Then sift in the flour, lifting your sieve quite high to incorporate air, and beat for 1–2 minutes until light and creamy. Divide the mixture evenly among the paper cases.
4. Bake in the preheated oven for 20–25 minutes until well risen and a skewer inserted into the middle of one of the cakes comes out clean. Remove from the oven and leave to cool in the tin for 10 minutes. Transfer to a wire rack to cool completely. Then, using an apple corer or cupcake corer, make a hole in the centre of the top of each cupcake. Spoon about 1 tbsp of rose petal jam to into the hole in each cupcake.

TO MAKE THE BUTTERCREAM:

1. Beat the butter until soft and creamy. Sift the icing sugar and add to the creamed butter in two additions mixing on a low speed alternating with the milk. Add the vanilla extract and beat for 3–5 minutes on a higher speed.
2. Divide the buttercream between two bowls. Mix in a little pink food colouring to half of the buttercream using a cocktail stick, leaving the other half white.
3. Spoon the white buttercream into a piping bag fitted with a star nozzle and swirl it on top of half the cupcakes. Fill a second piping bag with the pink buttercream and swirl it on top of the other half. Dust cupcakes with edible glitter and decorate with my handmade fondant roses and leaves (pages 22 and 110).

HOW TO MAKE
FONDANT ROSES

INGREDIENTS

Pink fondant icing

METHOD

1. Lay a large sheet of cling film on your work surface. Knead the fondant icing until it is pliable, then break off small pieces and roll between your hands to make little balls of different sizes. Place on the cling film.

2. Cover with another large sheet of cling film. Using your thumb, flatten each ball until quite thin. It doesn't matter if they are irregular sizes.

3. Peel off the top layer of cling film, start with the smallest piece of fondant icing and, using your fingers, gently roll the disc into a spiral to form the centre of the rose.

4. Take another petal and carefully wrap this around the central one, covering the seam.

5. As you add the petals, gently squeeze the edges to make them more shapely and curved. Continue until the rose is the size you want.

6. Pinch off any excess fondant icing from under the rose and stand it upright on some baking parchment. Continue until you have the number of roses you need, and then leave them for an hour to dry and firm.

RASPBERRY ICED TEA

Host a summer tea party and serve iced tea for summer rather than traditional hot tea. Try this fresh raspberry iced tea with some fresh floral ice cubes.

INGREDIENTS

2 litres (3½ pints) water
225g (8oz) sugar
1 punnet of raspberries
10 tea bags
60ml (2fl.oz) lemon juice

To serve:
My fresh floral ice cubes (page 114)

METHOD

1. Bring the water and sugar to a boil. Remove from the heat, and stir until the sugar is dissolved. Add the raspberries, tea bags and lemon juice. Cover and steep for 3 minutes then strain and discard berries and tea bags.

2. Transfer tea to a large jug. Refrigerate until chilled. Serve in pretty teapots, adding fresh floral ice cubes to the teacups.

FRESH FLORAL ICE CUBES

My fresh floral ice cubes are a pretty take on a regular ice cube. Make them using flowers picked from your garden. Be sure to use only organic, edible flowers that are pesticide and insect-free – although they are mainly for show, you need to make sure they are safe.

METHOD

1. Choose small flowers or roses. Rinse under a cold tap, leave to dry and trim off any extra foliage.
2. Bring some water to the boil. Let it cool completely.
3. Fill an ice cube tray about a quarter full. Place a flower face down in each compartment and freeze.
4. Take the cubes out of the freezer, gently fill the tray to the top with water and return to the freezer.
5. To serve, run warm water over the bottom of the tray to gently loosen the ice cubes.

MINI RASPBERRY, LEMON AND CHOCOLATE ÉCLAIRS

These French éclairs are perfect for a tea party.

(MAKES 10)

INGREDIENTS

For the choux pastry:

This French pastry is first cooked in a saucepan and then baked in a hot oven to make éclairs.

75g (3oz) plain flour

25g (1oz) butter

150ml (5fl.oz/¼ pint) water

2 eggs, beaten

For the filling:

150ml (5fl.oz/¼ pint) double cream, whipped

1 punnet of raspberries

For the chocolate glacé icing:

75g (3oz) icing sugar

25g (1oz) cocoa powder

2–3 tbsp water

¼ tsp vanilla extract

For the lemon glacé icing:

110g (4oz) icing sugar

2–3 tbsp lemon juice

Pink food colouring (gel/paste is best)

METHOD

1. Preheat the oven to 200°C/fan 180°C/400°F/gas mark 6 and grease and line two baking trays. Make the choux pastry. Sift the flour onto a piece of baking parchment. Melt the butter in the water in a small saucepan over a gentle heat. Bring the water to the boil, remove pan from heat and add the flour all at once.

2. Beat with a wooden spoon until the dough is smooth. Return the pan to moderate heat and continue beating until the dough forms a ball and leaves the sides of the pan clean. Do not overheat or the dough will become oily.

3. Cool the dough slightly and start adding the beaten eggs, a spoonful at a time. If the egg is added too quickly, the dough will become too slack and it will not be possible to pipe it. Spoon the choux pastry into a piping bag fitted with a 1.5cm/½ inch plain nozzle.

4. Pipe evenly spaced lines 7.5cm (3 inches) long a small distance apart, cutting off at each line with a knife.

5. Bake in the oven for 30–35 minutes until well risen, crisp and golden. When tapped they should sound hollow. Remove éclairs from the tray and make a slit in the side of each to allow steam to escape. When cold, fill with whipped cream and whole raspberries using a piping bag fitted with a plain nozzle.

TO MAKE THE CHOCOLATE GLACÉ ICING:

1. Sift the icing sugar with the cocoa powder into a bowl.

2. Mix in a spoonful of water at a time until the icing is of spreading consistency.

3. Flavour with vanilla extract. Spread the icing over half of the éclairs using a knife dipped in hot water.

TO MAKE THE LEMON GLACÉ ICING:
1. Sift the icing sugar into a bowl and mix in the lemon juice a tablespoon at a time until smooth.
2. Mix in a little of the pink food colouring using the tip of a cocktail stick. Spread over the other half of the éclairs. They should be eaten on the day you make them as the baked pastry becomes tough.

FONDANT FANCIES

Treat your friends and family to these fondant fancies presented with a pretty handmade fondant daisy on top.

(MAKES 9)

INGREDIENTS

For the cake:

110g (4oz) self-raising flour

110g (4oz) caster sugar

110g (4oz) butter, plus extra
  for greasing

1 tsp baking powder

2 eggs, beaten

1 tsp vanilla extract

For the buttercream:

75g (3oz) butter

25g (1oz) mascarpone

225g (8oz) icing sugar

1 tsp vanilla extract

For the icing:

350g (12oz) fondant icing
  sugar, sifted

4–5 tbsp water

Pastel colour food colouring(s)
(gel/paste is best)

For decorating:

White fondant icing

Yellow fondant icing

Daisy-shaped cutter

METHOD

1. Preheat the oven to 180°C/fan 160°C/350°F/gas mark 4. Grease a 15 x 15cm (6 x 6 inch) square cake tin and line the base with baking parchment.

2. Cream together the butter and sugar until pale and fluffy. Gradually whisk in the beaten eggs. Stir in the vanilla extract and sift the flour and baking powder over the mixture. Using a spatula, lightly fold in until thoroughly combined.

3. Pour mixture into the prepared cake tin. Level the top with a spatula and bake in the oven for 10–15 minutes until golden brown, and a skewer inserted into the middle of the cake comes out clean. Leave to cool in the tin for 10 minutes, then transfer to a wire rack.

4. While the cake is cooling, prepare the buttercream. Cream together the butter and mascarpone, then sift the icing sugar and add to the mixture. Mix until fully combined. Then mix in the vanilla extract.

5. Once your cake has cooled, trim the edges and cut into 5 x 5cm (2 x 2 inch) squares. Pipe a generous blob of buttercream onto the centre of each square and place onto a wire rack with baking parchment under it.

6. To make the icing, gradually mix the fondant icing sugar and water a tablespoon at a time until smooth and you have a runny icing. Divide the icing into small bowls and colour the icing with your chosen food colourings.

7. Generously spoon the icing over the square cakes until they are fully and evenly covered with a layer of icing. While the icing is still wet, gently place each cake into a cupcake case so it sticks. Allow to set.

8. Decorate as you like. I have used pretty daisies that I cut out using the yellow and white fondant icing.

ENGLISH MADELEINES

These retro cakes will be popular with your family on any occasion.

INGREDIENTS

110g (4oz) butter, plus extra
  for greasing
110g (4oz) caster sugar
2 eggs
110g (4oz) self-raising flour

To decorate:
Seedless raspberry jam
Desiccated coconut
Glacé cherries, halved

You will need:
6 x dariole moulds

METHOD

1. Preheat the oven to 180°C/fan 160°C/350°F/gas mark 4. Grease 6 dariole moulds with butter and dust with a little flour.
2. Cream the butter and sugar together into the bowl of a free-standing mixer (or you can use a handheld electric whisk and mixing bowl) until light and fluffy.
3. Beat each egg in separately.
4. Sift and then fold in the flour until well mixed.
5. Fill the dariole moulds until three-quarters full and bake on a baking tray or oven-proof dish for 20 minutes in the oven until firm to the touch, or a skewer inserted into the middle of one of the cakes comes out clean.
6. Remove from the oven and allow to cool in the tins for 5 minutes. Then carefully turn them out of the tins onto a wire rack (use a thin knife to help you).
7. When cool, trim the bottoms with a sharp knife so they are level and all stand at the same height.
8. In a saucepan, melt some seedless raspberry jam and brush it onto the madeleines.
9. Roll each cake in the coconut then finish by cutting a glacé cherry in half, dipping the cut side in some of the jam and placing on top of your madeleines.

CAKE POPS

Make these cake pops at your tea party or give them as a present in a gift bag tied with a bow. These heavenly bitesize cakes covered in white chocolate are a very special sweet treat for you and your guests.

(MAKES 20)

INGREDIENTS

110g (4oz) butter, plus extra
 for greasing
110g (4oz) caster sugar
110g (4oz) self-raising flour
2 eggs
1 tsp vanilla extract

For the buttercream:
110g (4oz) butter
225g (8oz) icing sugar, sifted

For decorating:
300g (10½oz) white chocolate
Food colourings (gel/pastes are
 best)
15cm (6 inch) lollipop sticks
Edible glitter
Handmade decorations (I have
 used moulds to make bows
 and flowers and cut out some
 butterflies, see page 22)

Amy's Tip

To make your cake pops secure before coating them with melted chocolate, it is important to chill them in the fridge after you have inserted the sticks.

METHOD

1. Preheat the oven to 180°C/fan 160°C/350°F/gas mark 4. Grease a 20cm (8 inch) cake tin and line the base with baking parchment.
2. Cream together the butter and sugar until light and fluffy. Add the eggs and vanilla extract then beat well to combine. Sift then fold in the flour.
3. Put the mixture in the tin and bake in the oven for 25 minutes until golden brown and well risen and a skewer inserted into one of the cakes comes out clean.
4. Transfer to a wire rack, gently peel off the baking parchment and cool completely. Once cooled, break into fine crumbs using your fingertips. Set aside.
5. Prepare the buttercream. Beat the butter until soft and creamy, then add the sifted icing sugar until mixed well. Add the buttercream to the cake crumbs and work together until the mix has the consistency of moist crumbs. Roll the mixture into 2.5cm (1 inch) diameter balls using your hands. Set onto a tray and chill for 1 hour.
6. Meanwhile, melt the white chocolate gently over a pan of simmering water. Once melted, transfer half to another container, adding a small amount of food colouring. Allow the chocolate to cool slightly for 10 minutes.
7. Dip the end of each lolly stick in the chocolate and insert one into each cake ball, about three-quarters of the way through. Chill for 15 minutes.
8. Dip the cake pops into the melted chocolate until fully coated. Push the cake pops into a block of polystyrene or acrylic cake pop stand (see Directory page 225).
9. Before the chocolate sets, sprinkle with edible glitter and top with pretty edible decorations.

MINI STRAWBERRIES AND CREAM CUPCAKES

Enjoy these bitesized fresh strawberry and whipped cream cakes, perfect for warm summer afternoons.

(MAKES 34)

INGREDIENTS

For the cupcakes:

110g (4oz) butter

110g (4oz) caster sugar

110g (4oz) self-raising flour

2 eggs

75g (3oz) strawberries cut into tiny pieces

For the strawberry cream:

600ml (20fl.oz/1 pint) double cream

150g (5oz) strawberries

1 tsp vanilla extract

1 tbsp icing sugar

To decorate:

Several strawberries, quartered

Amy's Tip

Why not try growing your own strawberries in strawberry pots to use in your recipes?

METHOD

1. Preheat the oven to 180°C/fan 160°C/350°F/gas mark 4 and line two mini muffin tins with mini muffin cases.

2. Put the butter, caster sugar, eggs and strawberry pieces into the bowl of a free-standing mixer (or you can use a handheld electric whisk and mixing bowl). Then sift in the flour, lifting your sieve quite high to incorporate air, then beat for 1–2 minutes until light and creamy.

3. Divide the mixture between the prepared mini muffin tins and bake in the oven for 20 minutes or until golden and well risen.

4. Meanwhile, in a small bowl, purée together your strawberries and icing sugar using a fork (or you can use a food processor).

5. Once the cakes are cooked, remove the cakes from the oven and leave to cool for 10 minutes before transferring them onto a wire rack to cool completely.

6. Meanwhile, prepare the strawberry cream. Whisk the cream, icing sugar and the vanilla extract into the bowl of a free-standing mixer using the whisk attachment (or you can use a handheld electric whisk and mixing bowl) until thick (take care not to over whisk) and lightly fold in the puréed strawberries.

7. Spoon into a piping bag fitted with a star nozzle and pipe the strawberry cream onto the cooled cakes.

8. Top each iced cake with a quarter of a strawberry.

HIGH TEA BISCUITS

Enjoy these beautiful and delicious shortbread biscuits with a cup of tea after all your hard work.

(MAKES 10)

INGREDIENTS

For the shortbread biscuits:
225g (8oz) plain flour
150g (5oz) butter, plus extra
 for greasing
50g (2oz) caster sugar

For the glacé icing:
500g (1lb 2oz) icing sugar, sifted
5–6 tbsp water
Few drops rosewater
Food colouring (gel/paste is best)

You will need:
Teacup-shaped cutter
Teapot-shaped cutter
Cocktail sticks

METHOD

1. Preheat the oven to 180°C/fan 160°C/350°F/gas mark 4 and lightly grease two baking trays. In the bowl of an electric mixer fitted with a paddle attachment, mix together the butter and sugar until combined. Sift in the flour and mix on a low speed until a dough forms. Lightly flour your work surface. Turn the dough out and knead into a flat disc. Wrap in cling film and chill for 30 minutes.

2. Roll out the dough to a thickness of 5mm (¼ inch) and use teacup and teapot cutters to cut out. Place on the prepared baking trays.

3. Bake in the preheated oven for 10–15 minutes or until a pale golden colour and the edges are browning. Remove from the oven, then cool on a wire rack.

4. When they have cooled, make the glacé icing. Mix the water and rosewater into the icing sugar a tablespoon at a time, and beat until smooth and you have a runny icing. Spoon a quarter of it into a separate bowl and colour with a small amount of pink food colouring using the tip of a cocktail stick. Spoon the pink icing into a small piping bag to outline and decorate the biscuits.

5. Make a small snip to the tip of another piping bag and turn the top half of the piping bag inside out. Place the piping bag in a tall glass or jug and pour the white icing in. Pipe a steady outline around each biscuit. Snip the piping bag again to make a slightly larger hole, then pipe and fill in (flood) the centres of the biscuits. Use a cocktail stick to carefully spread and fill in any gaps.

6. Use the pink icing in another piping bag to pipe on the outline and any patterns or polka dots. You can use edible pearls to decorate them as well for a finishing touch.

MINI PAVLOVAS

These delicate mini pavlovas, decorated with fresh berries, are perfect for summer to enjoy with friends and family.

(MAKES 18–20)

INGREDIENTS
3 egg whites
175g (6oz) caster sugar

To decorate:
300ml (10fl.oz/½ pint) double
  cream
1 tbsp icing sugar, plus extra
  for dusting
1 tsp vanilla extract
Fresh mixed berries

METHOD
1. Preheat the oven to 140°C/fan 120°C/275°F/gas mark 1 and line two baking trays with baking parchment.
2. For the meringues, place the egg whites in a clean dry bowl. Beat with the whisk attachment or an electric mixer until soft peaks form. Gradually add caster sugar, beating well between each addition. Beat until the mixture is thick and glossy.
3. Spoon heaped teaspoons of the mixture onto the lined baking trays. Slightly flatten and shape each one. Bake for 30–35 minutes or until crisp. Turn off the oven and cool completely in the oven with the door ajar.
4. Whisk together the cream, vanilla extract and icing sugar. Take care not to over whisk.
5. Arrange meringues on a serving dish and spoon the sweetened cream into the centre of each pavlova.
6. Decorate with fresh mixed berries. Using a tea strainer, dust with a little icing sugar. Serve immediately.

SCONES

A classic summertime favourite, ideal for afternoon tea. Make them even more delicious by making my strawberry jam to spread inside with clotted cream.

(MAKES 6)

INGREDIENTS
50g (2oz) butter, plus extra
 for greasing
pinch of salt
225g (8oz) self-raising flour
1 tsp baking powder
25g (1oz) caster sugar
100ml (3fl.oz) milk

For the egg wash:
1 egg
Few drops of milk

To serve:
Clotted cream
1 x jar shop-bought or homemade
 strawberry jam (page 74)

METHOD
1. Preheat the oven to 220°C/fan 200°C/425°F/gas mark 7, and lightly grease a baking tray.
2. Sift the flour and baking powder into a mixing bowl. Rub in the butter using the tips of your fingers, lifting your hands well above the bowl to incorporate as much air as possible. Stir in the sugar and salt. Make a well in the centre and pour in the milk. Use a knife to mix to a soft spongy dough. Turn onto a well-floured board and quickly knead out any cracks.
3. Pat out the dough and roll lightly with a floured rolling pin, until it is 3cm (1¼ inch) thick. Cut into rounds by pushing straight down tapping sharply into the dough with a floured scone cutter 6cm (2½ inch) wide. Take care not to twist the cutter or the scone will be out of shape. Put onto the prepared baking tray and glaze the top with egg wash (to make an egg wash, whisk the egg with a few drops of milk).
4. Bake near the top of the oven for around 15 minutes until the scones are well risen and golden brown. Remove from the oven and cool on a wire rack.
5. To serve, slice in half, and spread with strawberry jam and clotted cream.

Amy's Tip

As an alternative to an egg wash glossy top, you can dust with flour using a flour shaker for a soft crust.

BIRTHDAY CUPCAKES

These fun and pretty birthday cupcakes are great for parties and celebrating with friends and family of any age.

(MAKES 12)

INGREDIENTS

For the cupcakes:
175g (6oz) butter
175g (6oz) caster sugar
175g (6oz) self-raising flour
3 eggs
1 tsp vanilla extract

For the buttercream:
225g (8oz) butter
450g (1lb) icing sugar
1 tsp vanilla extract
1 tbsp milk
Yellow and pink food colourings
  (gel/paste is best)

You will need:
Coloured sprinkles and
  coloured sugar
Birthday candles

METHOD

1. Preheat the oven to 180°C/fan 160°C/350°F/gas mark 4 and line a 12-hole muffin tin with paper cupcake or muffin cases.

2. Put the butter, caster sugar, eggs and vanilla extract into the bowl of a free-standing electric mixer (or you can use a handheld electric whisk and mixing bowl). Then sift in the flour, lifting your sieve quite high to incorporate air, and beat for 1–2 minutes until light and creamy. Divide the mixture evenly between the paper cases.

3. Bake in the preheated oven for 20–25 minutes, or until well risen and a skewer inserted into one of the cakes comes out clean. Remove from the oven and leave to cool in the tin for 10 minutes. Transfer to a wire rack to cool completely.

4. Meanwhile, prepare the buttercream. Put the butter into the bowl of a free-standing electric mixer (or you can use a handheld electric whisk and mixing bowl) and beat until soft and creamy.

5. Sift the icing sugar and add to the creamed butter in two additions on a low speed incorporating the vanilla extract and milk, then beat again for 3–5 minutes on a higher speed.

6. Divide the buttercream into three bowls. Add pink food colouring to one, and yellow food colouring to another using the tip of a cocktail stick. Leave the rest of the icing white.

7. Spoon the butter icing into a piping bag fitted with a star nozzle and swirl onto the top of the cupcakes.

8. Decorate with the coloured sprinkles and sugars.

Father's Day

Show your dad how much you love him by baking him a chocolate cake – a favourite treat of my dad's – or my fun Shirt and Tie Biscuits.

Shirt and Tie Biscuits   136

Chocolate Celebration Cake   138

SHIRT AND TIE BISCUITS

These shirt and tie biscuits are a fun gift to give your dad this Father's Day.

(MAKES 10)

INGREDIENTS

For the shortbread biscuits:
225g (8oz) plain flour
150g (5oz) butter, plus extra
  for greasing
50g (2oz) caster sugar
1 vanilla pod (seeds only)

For the glacé icing:
500g (1lb 2oz) icing sugar, sifted
5–6 tbsp water
Food colourings (gel/paste is best)

To decorate:
White fondant icing

You will need:
Shirt-shaped cutter
Cocktail sticks

METHOD

1. Preheat the oven to 180°C/fan 160°C/350°F/gas mark 4 and lightly grease two baking trays.
2. In a bowl of an electric mixer, mix the butter and sugar until combined.
3. Split the vanilla pod with a sharp knife and scrape the seeds from the pod (saving the skin). Add the vanilla seeds and continue to mix. Sift in the flour and mix on a low speed until a dough forms. Lightly flour your work surface. Turn the dough out and knead into a flat disc. Wrap in cling film and chill for 30 minutes.
4. Roll out the dough to a thickness of 5mm (¼ inch) and cut out using a shirt-shaped cutter. Use a palette knife to lift and transfer biscuits to the prepared baking trays.
5. Bake in the preheated oven for 10–15 minutes or until a pale golden colour and the edges are browning. Remove from the oven, then leave on a wire rack to cool.

TO DECORATE:

1. Gradually mix the water into the icing sugar a tablespoon at a time and beat until smooth and you have a runny icing. Save some glacé icing for the sugar ties.
2. Make a small snip to the tip of a piping bag and turn the top half of the piping bag inside out. Place the piping bag into a tall glass or jug and fill with the white icing. Pipe a steady outline around each biscuit. Snip the tip of the piping bag again to make a slightly larger hole, and pipe and fill in (flood) the centres of the biscuits.
3. Roll out a small amount of fondant icing thinly and cut out little tie shapes with a sharp knife. Use some of the glacé icing you saved and add bright food colourings to it using the tip of a cocktail stick. Spoon this icing into a small piping bag, and pipe fun designs onto your ties. Stick them to the shirts with a little more icing.

CHOCOLATE CELEBRATION CAKE

Show your dad how much you love and appreciate him this Father's Day and bake him this rich velvety chocolate cake.

(SERVES 8–10)

INGREDIENTS

300g (11oz) dark chocolate

525g (1lb 2oz) butter, plus extra
   for greasing

700g (1lb 8oz) caster sugar

12 eggs

300g (11oz) self-raising flour

75g (3oz) cocoa powder

For the chocolate buttercream:

400g (14oz) butter

1kg (2lb 2oz) icing sugar

125g (4½oz) cocoa powder

150ml (5fl.oz/¼ pint) milk

For the vanilla buttercream:

110g (4oz) butter

225g (8oz) icing sugar

1 tsp milk

1 tsp vanilla extract

To decorate:

1 punnet fresh blueberries

5–6 chocolate flakes, crumbled

You will need:

3 x 20cm (8 inch) round cake tins

METHOD

1. Preheat the oven to 180°C/fan 160°C/350°F/gas mark 4, and lightly grease 3 x 20cm (8 inch) cake tins and line the base of each with baking parchment.

2. Melt the butter and chocolate in a heatproof bowl over a pan of simmering water. Stir until completely melted and glossy. Remove from the heat and leave to cool for 10 minutes.

3. Beat the chocolate and butter in the bowl of a free-standing electric mixer for 3 minutes. Add the sugar and continue to beat for 1 minute. Beat in the eggs one at a time. Sift the flour and cocoa powder and add to the mixture in three additions. Beat until well incorporated.

4. Divide the mixture between your three prepared 8 inch (20cm) cake tins. Bake in the preheated oven for 25–30 minutes until well risen and a skewer inserted into the middle of the cakes comes out clean. Remove from the oven and leave for 10 minutes before removing from tins. Remove the baking parchment and leave to cool on a wire rack before icing and decorating.

5. While the cakes are cooling, prepare the chocolate buttercream. Beat the butter until soft and creamy. Sift the icing sugar and cocoa and add to the butter in three additions, beating on low speed between each addition. Now gradually add the milk on a slow speed. When mixed in, beat on a higher speed for 3–5 minutes until creamy and smooth.

6. When the cakes are completely cool, place one layer in the centre of a single-tiered cake stand or plate. Using a palette knife, spread some buttercream onto the top of the cake layer to about 1cm thick then repeat this with the next layer of the cake. When your three layers of cake have been placed on top of each other, spread the remaining chocolate buttercream over the top and sides of the cake until fully covered and smooth the top using a palette knife.

7. Crumble up the flakes and gently press the pieces around the side of the three-layered cake.

8. Make the vanilla buttercream to edge the top of the cake. Beat the butter until soft and creamy. Sift the icing sugar into the butter in two additions on a low speed. When incorporated, slowly add the milk and vanilla extract still on a low speed. When mixed in, beat for 3–5 minutes on a higher speed.

9. Spoon the vanilla buttercream into a piping bag fitted with a star nozzle to pipe a shell pattern around the border on the top of your cake. For a finishing touch use fresh blueberries to decorate the top of your cake like I have.

AUTUMN

Halloween

This can be a fun, exciting time of the year for children. Why not throw them a party with their friends to decorate their own chocolate-covered apples?

Cinnamon Sugar Doughnuts   144

Chocolate Apples   147

Chocolate Orange Whoopie Pies   148

Toffee Apple Jam   150

Toffee Apple Cupcakes   151

Spiced Pumpkin Bundt Cake   154

CINNAMON SUGAR DOUGHNUTS

Hang from string as a Halloween game for children.

(MAKES 10–15)

INGREDIENTS

375g (13oz) plain flour
225g (8oz) caster sugar
2 tsp baking powder
1 tsp salt
½ tsp ground cinnamon
½ tsp ground cloves
¼ tsp ground nutmeg
2 eggs
1 tsp vanilla extract
1 tsp butter
1 tsp lard or vegetable shortening
250ml (8fl.oz) milk
Caster sugar and cinnamon
  to decorate

You will need:
Doughnut batter dispenser
  (see Directory page 225)

METHOD

1. Beat the eggs in a mixing bowl, then add the butter, lard, vanilla extract, sugar and milk and beat together.
2. In a separate bowl, sift together all the dry ingredients. Add the dry ingredients to the egg mixture, beating until smooth.
3. Fill the doughnut batter dispenser with batter.
4. In a large saucepan, heat the vegetable oil until it reaches 185°C/365°F on a thermometer. Press the dispenser to release the batter into the oil and deep fry until golden brown on each side. Repeat this process for each doughnut.
5. Once the doughnuts have been fried, place them onto kitchen roll to remove some of the oil, then roll them in caster sugar mixed with cinnamon. They are best when served just after frying.

> *Amy's Tip*
> If you do not have a doughnut batter dispenser, you can use a spoon or ice cream scoop to make doughnuts without a hole.

CHOCOLATE APPLES

These fun Halloween treats are a great alternative to toffee apples.

(MAKES 6)

INGREDIENTS

6 Granny Smith apples

450g (1lb) milk chocolate

225g (8oz) white chocolate
 to decorate

Lollipop sticks

METHOD

1. Wash and dry the apples and insert the sticks into the cores. Melt the milk chocolate and white chocolate in separate heatproof bowls over a pan of simmering water.

2. Dip the apples into the chocolate, making sure they are fully coated. Place on baking parchment and leave to set before using a piping bag to pipe on stripes, or alternatively dip in chopped nuts, sprinkles or sweets while wet.

3. Tie a bow around each stick before serving.

CHOCOLATE ORANGE WHOOPIE PIES

These rich chocolate cake halves are the perfect match with this fluffy zingy orange buttercream.

(MAKES 15)

INGREDIENTS
175g (6oz) plain flour

100g (3½oz) cocoa powder

1 tsp baking powder

125g (4½oz) butter, plus extra
  for greasing

200g (7oz) caster sugar

1 egg

225ml (8fl.oz) buttermilk

1 tsp vanilla extract

For the buttercream:

100g (3oz) butter

225g (8oz) icing sugar, sifted

Zest of 1 orange

METHOD
1. Preheat the oven to 180°C/fan 160°C/350°F/gas mark 4.
2. Line two baking trays with baking parchment.
3. Sift the flour, cocoa powder and baking powder into a bowl. Stir together.
4. Cream together the butter and sugar into a bowl of a free-standing electric mixer (or you can use a handheld electric whisk and mixing bowl), then beat in the egg until fully incorporated. Mix in the buttermilk and vanilla.
5. Slowly add the sifted dry ingredients to the wet ingredients in two additions. Chill the mixture for 30 minutes.
6. Once chilled, use a piping bag fitted with a 1cm (½ inch) nozzle to pipe circles of mixture onto the baking trays, leaving a few centimetres between each one.
7. Bake for 10 minutes, and then allow to cool completely on a wire rack.
8. While they are cooling, beat together the butter and icing sugar into the bowl of a free-standing mixer (or you can use a handheld electric mixer and mixing bowl) until soft and creamy. Add the orange zest and mix until fully incorporated.
9. Once the cake halves are cooled, spread or pipe a generous amount of the orange buttercream onto one half and sandwich it together with another half. Repeat this until you have filled all of your whoopie pies.

TOFFEE APPLE JAM

To fill your toffee apple cupcakes.

INGREDIENTS

For the toffee sauce:

110g (4oz) light muscovado sugar

4 tbsp golden syrup

110g (4oz) butter

4 tbsp double cream

For the apple jam:

450g (1lb) Bramley apples
  (cored and peeled)

75ml (3 fl.oz) water

1 vanilla pod

2 tbsp lemon juice

200g (7oz) white granulated sugar

Amy's Tip

Keep the saved vanilla pod cut in three and put in a jar of sugar to make delicately flavoured vanilla sugar.

METHOD

1. To make the toffee sauce, melt the sugar, syrup and butter in a small saucepan and slowly bring to the boil. Reduce the heat and simmer for about 3 minutes or until thick. Stir in the cream, remove from the heat and leave to cool.

2. To make the apple jam, place the apples, water, vanilla pod and lemon juice in a large pan and cook down for about 15–20 minutes until soft. Save the vanilla pod.

3. Once the apples have become soft and fluffy, add the sugar and cook over a low heat until the sugar has dissolved. Then turn up the heat and bring to a boil for 4–5 minutes until the jam is thick.

4. Remove from the heat and stir the prepared toffee sauce into the apple jam and leave to cool ready to fill the toffee apple cupcakes.

5. After filling the cored cupcakes you can put any extra jam into sterilised jars.

TOFFEE APPLE CUPCAKES

These cupcakes, filled with toffee apple jam, are a fun treat for autumn-time and Bonfire Night, resembling toffee apples drenched with gleaming toffee sauce.

(MAKES 12)

INGREDIENTS
For the cupcakes:
175g (6oz) butter
175g (6oz) caster sugar
175g (6oz) self-raising flour
3 eggs
1 tsp vanilla extract

For the filling:
Toffee apple jam (page 150)

For the toffee sauce:
110g (4oz) light muscovado sugar
4 tbsp golden syrup
110g (4oz) butter
4 tbsp double cream

For the toffee buttercream:
¼ vanilla pod, seeds only
225g (8oz) butter
450g (1lb) icing sugar
2 tbsp toffee sauce
¼ tsp vanilla extract

You will need:
12 lolly sticks

METHOD
1. Prepare the toffee apple jam (page 150).
2. Preheat the oven to 180°C/fan 160°C/350°F/gas mark 4 and line a 12-hole muffin tray with paper cupcake or muffin cases.
3. Put the butter, caster sugar, eggs and vanilla extract into the bowl of a free-standing electric mixer (or you can use a handheld electric whisk and mixing bowl). Sift in the flour, lifting your sieve quite high to incorporate air, and beat for 1–2 minutes until light and creamy.
4. Divide the mixture evenly between the paper cases and bake in the oven for 25 minutes or until golden and well risen and a skewer inserted into one of the cakes comes out clean. Remove from the oven and leave to cool in the tin for 10 minutes. Transfer to a wire rack to cool completely.
5. Once cooled, make a small cut to the tip of a piping bag with scissors. Turn the top half of the bag inside out, and use a spatula to fill it with the toffee apple jam. Using an apple corer, make a hole in the centre of the top of each cupcake, being careful not to push the corer through the bottom of the cake.
6. Squeeze enough toffee apple jam to fill the hole you have made in each cupcake.

TO MAKE THE TOFFEE SAUCE:
1. Melt the sugar, syrup and butter in a small saucepan and slowly bring to the boil.
2. Reduce the heat and simmer for about 3 minutes, or until thick.
3. Stir in the cream, remove from the heat and leave to cool.

TO MAKE THE TOFFEE BUTTERCREAM:

1. Slice the vanilla pod in half lengthwise and scrape out the seeds. Save the seeds, and set the pod aside.
2. Beat the butter in the bowl of a free-standing electric mixer on medium speed (or you can use a handheld electric whisk and mixing bowl) until creamy.
3. Add the vanilla seeds and mix for a few seconds on medium speed.
4. In a separate bowl, sift the icing sugar.
5. Add the icing sugar to the butter mixture on low speed until it begins to incorporate.
6. Warm the toffee sauce (make sure it is warm not hot).
7. Add 2 tbsp of the warmed toffee sauce and vanilla extract, and beat at medium speed until fully incorporated.
8. Spoon the toffee buttercream into a piping bag fitted with a plain nozzle and swirl it on top of the cupcakes.
9. Drizzle with the remaining gleaming, melted and cooled toffee sauce. Transform your cupcakes into toffee apples by inserting a lolly stick into the centre of each cupcake.

SPICED PUMPKIN BUNDT CAKE

Make this simple and beautiful autumn-themed Halloween dessert look special by decorating it with fresh autumnal flowers and berries from your garden for the whole family to enjoy.

(SERVES 12)

INGREDIENTS

475g (1lb 1oz) plain flour
2 tsp baking powder
1 tsp bicarbonate of soda
2 tsp ground cinnamon
1½ tsp ground cloves
1 tsp ground mixed spice
1 tsp ground nutmeg
¼ tsp salt
410g (14¼oz) granulated sugar
250ml (8fl.oz) vegetable oil
4 eggs
1 x 425g (15oz) tin pumpkin purée

For the cream cheese frosting:
75g (3oz) butter
225g (8oz) cream cheese
175g (6oz) icing sugar, sifted
3-4 tbsp milk, plus more if needed

To decorate:
Small flowers and autumn berries

Amy's Tip

Look in your garden for autumnal flowers or berries, making sure they are non-poisonous and insect-free.

METHOD

1. Preheat the oven to 180°C/fan 160°C/350°F/gas mark 4 and lightly grease a bundt or ring cake tin with butter or a flavourless oil spray.

2. Sift the flour, baking powder, bicarbonate of soda, cinnamon, cloves, mixed spice, nutmeg and salt into a large bowl and mix together.

3. Beat the sugar and vegetable oil in the bowl of a free standing electric mixer fitted with a paddle attachment (or you can use a handheld electric whisk and mixing bowl) on a medium speed for 1–2 minutes or until the sugar is incorporated. Scrape down the sides of the bowl and paddle with a spatula. Add the eggs one at a time, beating well after each addition. Reduce the speed and add the pumpkin and beat until combined.

4. On a low speed, add the flour mixture in two additions and beat on a higher speed for 1–2 minutes until fully incorporated.

5. Pour the mixture into the prepared tin and bake for 1 hour until a skewer inserted into the cake comes out clean. Leave for 5 minutes before turning out of the tin onto a wire rack and leave to cool completely.

6. For the cream cheese frosting, beat the butter in the bowl of a free-standing electric mixer (or you can use a handheld electric whisk and mixing bowl) until soft and creamy, then beat in the cream cheese, icing sugar and milk until you reach a pouring consistency.

7. When the cake has cooled completely, place on a cake stand. Put the icing in a jug and pour over the top of the cake, allowing it to drip down the sides.

8. Decorate with fresh autumn flowers and berries.

Autumn/Bonfire Night

Stay inside to watch the fireworks on Bonfire Night and tuck into a sticky toffee pudding. Just add a sparkler!

Autumn Leaf Biscuits   158

Mulled Cider   161

Autumn Chutney   162

Sticky Toffee Puddings   164

Apple, Blackberry and Plum Pie   167

Hot Cocoa with Homemade Marshmallows   168

AUTUMN LEAF BISCUITS

When I was little, my mum, my sister Lara and I baked biscuits together for every season and occasion. Inspired by our lovely garden, depicting warm autumn colours, these were a favourite of ours.

(MAKES 20)

INGREDIENTS

For the biscuits:
110g (4oz) butter
110g (4oz) dark muscovado sugar
60g (2½oz) maple syrup
300g (11oz) plain flour
1 tsp bicarbonate of soda
1 tsp cinnamon

For the maple glacé icing:
225g (8oz) icing sugar, sifted
2 tbsp maple syrup

You will need:
Assorted leaf-shaped biscuit
  cutters
Small piping bag
Cocktail sticks

METHOD

1. Preheat the oven to 200°C/fan 180°C/400°F/gas mark 6 and line two baking trays with baking parchment.
2. Melt the butter, sugar and syrup in a small saucepan and let it cool.
3. Sift the flour, bicarbonate of soda and cinnamon into a large bowl and stir in the melted butter mixture until it becomes a stiff dough.
4. Roll the dough out onto baking parchment to a thickness of 5mm (¼ inch) and cut the dough into leaf shapes using assorted leaf-shaped biscuits cutters.
5. Using a palette knife carefully lift and transfer your leaves to the baking trays. Bake for 10–12 minutes until hard then remove from the oven and cool on a wire rack.
6. Mix together the icing sugar and maple syrup in a bowl and beat until smooth. If it is too thin add some more icing sugar, if it is too thick add more maple syrup.
7. Separate the icing into small bowls and add orange, red and yellow food colouring with a cocktail stick until you have the colours you want. Turn the top half of the piping bag inside out and place into a tall glass or jug and fill with icing. Make a small snip to the tip of the piping bag and pipe a steady outline around each biscuit. Snip the tip of the piping bag again to make a slightly larger hole, and pipe and fill in (flood) the centres of the biscuits. Use a cocktail stick to carefully spread and fill in any gaps up to the piped outline, being careful not to let the icing over flow around the edges. If you like, you can ice some of them with melted chocolate as I have.
8. Once you have iced them and they have set, you can now pipe veins onto them using a small piping bag so they look like real leaves.

Цена 1 р. 75 к.

MULLED CIDER

Instead of a glass or mug, core out apples to serve this warming drink.

(SERVES 8–10)

INGREDIENTS

2 litres (3½ pints) dry cider or
  fresh apple juice
2 apples studded with cloves
4–6 cinnamon sticks
2 star anise
Juice and zest of 1 orange
Apples, to serve

METHOD

1. Combine all ingredients in a large saucepan and simmer gently for 30 minutes.
2. Transfer to a heatproof bowl.
3. To serve, slice the tops off the apples. Remove and discard the cores. Pour the cider into the apple cups. Add a cinnamon stick and a star anise to each cup to decorate.

AUTUMN CHUTNEY

Perfect as a gift or to enjoy yourself with cheese and biscuits.

(MAKES 8 JARS)·

INGREDIENTS

725g (1lb 10oz) apples, peeled,
  cored and cubed
1kg (2lb 2oz) pears, peeled, cored,
  chopped and cubed
500g (1lb 2oz) fresh figs, cut in
  quarters
375g (13oz) onions, peeled
  and diced
1 tbsp ground cinnamon
1 tbsp cardamom seeds
1 tsp mace
Zest and juice of 2 oranges
500g (1lb 2oz) soft dark
  brown sugar
500ml (16fl.oz) cider vinegar

METHOD

1. Sterilise the jars. First wash them in warm soapy water and rinse. Allow them to drip dry, upside down on a rack in the oven set to 180°C/fan 160°C/350°F/gas mark 4 for 5 minutes (or you can carefully swill the washed jars with boiled water).

2. Place the prepared onions, apples, pears and figs into a large pan with the orange juice and simmer until the onions and fruit have cooked and have broken down. Add the spices, orange zest, vinegar and sugar. Bring to a boil and then reduce the heat and simmer for about 30 minutes until the chutney has thickened.

3. Ladle the chutney into the sterilised jars and seal. Store in a cool dark place and give as a gift or serve with bread and cheese.

STICKY TOFFEE PUDDINGS

Smother these little classic puddings with toffee sauce and top with sparklers for Bonfire Night.

(MAKES 6)

INGREDIENTS

75g (3oz) butter, plus extra
  for greasing
150g (5oz) caster sugar
175g (6oz) self-raising flour
2 eggs, beaten
175g (6oz) stoned dates
175ml (6fl.oz) boiling water
½ tsp vanilla extract
3 tsps black coffee (or Kahlúa)
1 tsp bicarbonate of soda

For the sauce:
175g (6oz) soft dark brown sugar
110g (4oz) butter
7 tbsp double cream
50g (2oz) walnuts, chopped

To serve:
Double cream

You will need:
6 x mini pudding tins

METHOD

1. Preheat the oven to 180°C/fan 160°C/350°F/gas mark 4.

2. Roughly chop the dates and put them in a bowl. Pour the boiling water over them and then add the vanilla extract, coffee and bicarbonate of soda and leave to one side.

3. Cream the butter and sugar in a free-standing electric mixer (or you can use a handheld electric whisk and mixing bowl) until the mixture is pale and fluffy. Add the beaten eggs, a little at a time, beating well between each addition.

4. Sift the flour and lightly fold it into the mixture, followed by the date mixture.

5. Grease 6 mini pudding tins with butter, and line the bases with a cut out disc of baking parchment. Divide the mixture equally between them three-quarters full. Place on a baking tray and bake in the oven for 25 minutes.

6. When removed from the oven, leave to cool for 5 minutes before turning each pudding out of its tin. Peel off the baking parchment. If you need to, slice a little off the bottom of each pudding so they are level and sit evenly on a plate.

7. To make the sauce, place the butter and sugar in a saucepan and heat gently until melted and combined. Add the cream and stir until fully incorporated. Stir in the chopped walnuts.

8. To serve, pour the toffee sauce over each pudding and drizzle each pudding with cream.

APPLE, BLACKBERRY AND PLUM PIE

Perfect to enjoy on a chilly Sunday afternoon with cream or homemade ice cream.

(SERVES 6)

INGREDIENTS

For the pastry:
275g (10oz) plain flour
75g (3oz) caster sugar
175g (3oz) butter, cubed
1 egg yolk
1–2 tbsp cold water

For the filling:
2 Granny Smith/green apples
3 plums
Handful of blackberries
100g (3½oz) dark muscovado sugar
75ml (3fl.oz) freshly squeezed
   orange juice

For the egg wash:
1 egg
Few drops of milk

METHOD

1. Combine the flour, sugar and butter in a food processor until the mixture resembles fine breadcrumbs. Add the egg yolk and enough water for the pastry to come together. Wrap in cling film and chill for 30 minutes.

2. Preheat the oven to 180°C/fan 160°C/350°F/gas mark 4. Core the apples, cut them into slices and cut them in half. Stone the plums and quarter them. Put the apples, plums and blackberries into a heatproof oven dish and mix in the sugar and orange juice. Bake for 25–30 minutes until the fruit is tender.

3. Once cooked remove most of the syrup and set aside for serving later. Turn the oven up to 190°C/fan 170°C/375°F/gas mark 5.

4. Grease a 20cm (8 inch) tart tin with butter. Roll out two thirds of the pastry onto a floured surface until it is 3mm (⅛ inch) thick. Carefully lay the pastry over the rolling pin, then drape over the tin leaving a little hanging over the edge.

5. Fill the pie shell with the fruit mixture. To create the lattice top, roll out the remaining pastry and cut into strips 1cm (½ inch) wide. Lay the strips over the filling, weaving to form a lattice. Trim and seal the edges with water. Use your fingers to crimp around the rim, then glaze the top with the egg wash. Sprinkle with a little sugar, and bake for 45 minutes or until golden. Serve with ice cream and the reserved syrup.

HOT COCOA WITH HOMEMADE MARSHMALLOWS

Homemade marshmallows are the perfect addition to hot cocoa to warm you up this autumn.

(MAKES ABOUT 20 MARSHMALLOWS)

INGREDIENTS

For the marshmallows:
9 sheets leaf gelatine
450g (1lb) caster sugar
1 tbsp liquid glucose
200ml (7fl.oz) water
2 egg whites
1 tsp vanilla extract
Icing sugar
Cornflour

For the cocoa (serves 2):
1 tbsp cocoa powder
2 tbsp icing sugar
600ml (20fl.oz/1 pint) milk

TO MAKE THE MARSHMALLOWS:

1. Lightly oil a shallow baking tray and dust it with sieved icing sugar and cornflour.
2. Soak the gelatine in 140ml (4fl.oz) of the cold water.
3. Put the remaining water in a heavy-based pan with the sugar and glucose. Bring to the boil and continue cooking for 12–15 minutes until the temperature reaches 127°C on a sugar thermometer.
4. When the sugar reaches the temperature, carefully add the gelatine and the water to the syrup. Pour the syrup into a metal bowl or jug.
5. Whisk the egg whites until stiff using an electric whisk in a mixing bowl. Pour in the syrup and continue to whisk. The mixture will start to thicken. Add the vanilla extract and continue whisking for 5–10 minutes until the mixture is stiff and thick enough to hold its shape on the whisk.
6. Spoon the mixture into the prepared tin and smooth with a wet palette knife.
7. Leave for at least 2 hours to set.
8. Dust the work surface with icing sugar and cornflour. Loosen the marshmallow around the sides of the pan with a knife and turn it out onto the dusted surface.
9. Cut into squares and roll in the sugar and cornflour. Leave to dry on a wire rack.

TO MAKE THE COCOA:

1. Place the cocoa powder and icing sugar into a small saucepan, add the milk and whisk to combine.
2. Heat until hot and divide between two mugs. Serve with homemade marshmallows.

WINTER

Christmas

I love Christmas – it is my favourite time of year. The run-up to Christmas is so exciting and magical, planning what treats I will make over the festive period to entertain family and friends. Making a gingerbread house from scratch, a traditional Christmas cake and crumbly mince pies are just a few family Christmas traditions in my home.

Instead of hunting in the cold for gifts for family and friends, why not spend winter planning and preparing edible gifts that they are sure to love, in the comfort of your home?

Gingerbread House   176

Stained Glass Window Biscuits   180

Christmas Cake   182

Mince Pies   185

Mincemeat   188

Red Velvet Angel Cupcakes   190

Christmas Baked Alaska   193

Candy Cane Biscuits   196

Snowflake Biscuits   198

Salted Caramel Peanut Butter Cups   201

Red Velvet Cupcake Ice Cream   202

New Year's Eve Cupcake Clock   205

'I'VE FOUND THAT FAMILY AND FRIENDS REALLY APPRECIATE THE THOUGHT THAT GOES INTO HOMEMADE EDIBLE GIFTS. SO WHY NOT SPEND THE WINTER MONTHS PLANNING AND PREPARING BAKED TREATS, BEAUTIFULLY PACKAGED, THAT PEOPLE ARE SURE TO LOVE?'

GINGERBREAD HOUSE

This gingerbread house looks beautiful and tastes delicious if you can bear to break it apart after using it for decoration. It is a fun activity for families to make together when it's cold outside.

INGREDIENTS

375g (13oz) butter
275g (10oz) brown sugar
3 egg yolks
750g (1lb 11oz) plain flour
3 tsp bicarbonate soda
9 tsp ground ginger
7½ tbsp golden syrup

Gingerbread house template
 (page 179)

For the royal icing:
700g (1lb 8oz) icing sugar, sifted
3 egg whites
3 tsp lemon juice

For the decoration:
Candy canes
Orange and red boiled sweets
Icing sugar for dusting

METHOD

1. Preheat the oven to 180°C/fan 160°C/350°F/gas mark 4. Cream the butter and sugar until light and fluffy. Add the egg yolks and beat well. Gradually add the sifted dry ingredients and syrup and mix well. Knead the dough lightly and divide it into portions for rolling out.

2. Roll out the dough onto baking parchment to 5mm (¼ inch) thick. Use my template to help you cut out the structure of the house with a knife. If there is any dough left, make a gingerbread family using gingerbread people cutters. Line several baking trays with baking parchment and carefully place all parts onto the baking trays. Cut out two small square-shaped windows into the sides of the house and the front, leaving room in the middle of the front for the front door. Cut out a heart from the front like I have and place a red boiled sweet in it onto the baking tray. Place orange boiled sweets in the windows onto the baking trays. Bake for 10 minutes until browned and hardened. Cool on a wire rack. Gently cut out a door on the front in between the two windows while still warm, and leave covered overnight to harden and dry out ready for assembling your gingerbread house.

3. The next day, make your royal icing which will act as a cement to stick your house together and to decorate your house and gingerbread family. In a bowl, using the whisk attachment of an electric mixer, beat the egg whites until frothy. Add the sifted icing sugar gradually, beating well between each addition. Then beat in lemon juice until thickened and at a piping consistency.

4. Fill a small piping bag with the royal icing and snip a small hole at the end. Before sticking the house together,

you need to decorate the roof and pipe on the window panes. Once this has dried, get a plate or cake stand for your gingerbread house to sit on. Cut a large snip into your piping bag that is filled with royal icing. Start by piping the icing onto the edges of each side, front and back and the bottom of each piece to stick them to the board, then leave for 1 hour to set.

5. When you have stuck all of the walls together, carefully stick the first half of the roof on. Hold in place until it has set, then repeat on the other side. Leave to set for a few hours. Now stick the chimney on using icing.

6. Finish by piping more icing around the house and on the roof and chimney to look like snow. Decorate with candy canes and boiled sweets for the roof. Place the door in position and finally, dust with icing sugar to look like freshly fallen snow.

House   1 square equals 1"/2.5cm

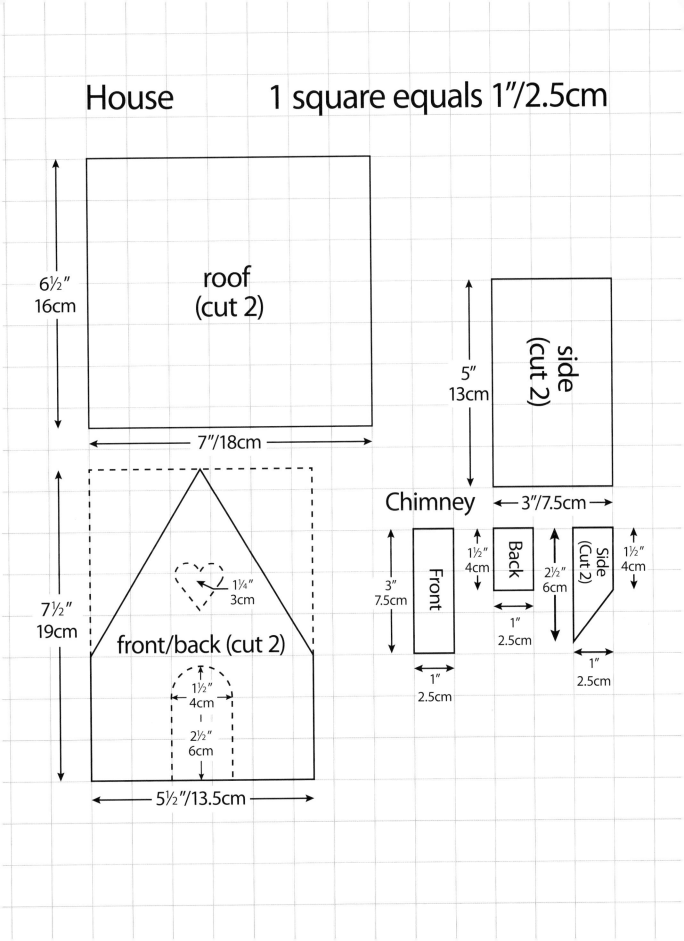

roof
(cut 2)

6½"
16cm

7"/18cm

side
(cut 2)

5"
13cm

3"/7.5cm

Chimney

front/back (cut 2)

7½"
19cm

1¼"
3cm

1½"
4cm

2½"
6cm

5½"/13.5cm

Front

3"
7.5cm

1"
2.5cm

Back

1½"
4cm

1"
2.5cm

Side
(Cut 2)

2½"
6cm

1½"
4cm

1"
2.5cm

STAINED GLASS WINDOW BISCUITS

Hang these beautiful stained glass biscuits on your tree this Christmas.

(MAKES 20)

INGREDIENTS

110g (4oz) butter
60g (2½oz) light soft brown sugar
1 egg yolk
350g (12oz) plain flour
1 tsp bicarbonate soda
3 tsp ginger
1 tsp cinnamon
2½ tbsp golden syrup
Brightly coloured boiled sweets

METHOD

1. Preheat the oven to 180°C/fan 160°C/350°F/gas mark 4. Cream the butter and sugar in the bowl of a free-standing electric mixer (or you can use a handheld electric whisk and mixing bowl) until light and fluffy. Add the egg yolk and beat well. Gradually add the sifted dry ingredients and the syrup and mix well.

2. Line two baking trays with baking parchment. Roll your dough onto a floured surface to a thickness of 5mm (¼ inch) and cut out using star, heart or other Christmas cutter shapes. In the middle of each biscuit cut out a smaller shape using a smaller cutter. Use a straw to make a small hole in the top of each biscuit ready to hang later. Lay them on your prepared baking trays and place a boiled sweet in the middle of each biscuit where you have cut out a smaller shape. This will melt in the oven to create the 'stained glass' window effect.

3. Bake in the preheated oven for 10 minutes. Remove from the oven and leave the biscuits on the baking trays until the 'stained glass' has set.

4. Thread your cooled biscuits with narrow ribbon or string and hang on your Christmas tree.

CHRISTMAS CAKE

Christmas wouldn't be the same without a traditional Christmas cake.

(SERVES 10–12)

INGREDIENTS
450g (1lb) currants
200g (7oz) sultanas
200g (7oz) raisins
75g (3oz) glacé cherries, rinsed,
  dried and finely chopped
75g (3oz) mixed candied peel,
  finely chopped
100ml (3fl.oz) of brandy plus 2 tbsp
  for 'feeding' the cake
225g (8oz) plain flour
1 tsp freshly grated nutmeg
1 tsp ground mixed spice
1 tsp ground cinnamon
225g (8oz) butter, plus extra
  for greasing
225g (8oz) soft brown sugar
4 eggs
60g (2½oz) almonds, sliced
60g (2½oz) ground almonds
1 tbsp black treacle
Grated zest of 1 orange
Grated zest and juice of 1 lemon

You will need:
20cm (8 inch) round cake tin,
  greased and lined with baking
  parchment

METHOD
1. Place the dried fruit, mixed peel, lemon zest, orange zest, lemon juice and brandy in a large bowl. Cover with a clean cloth and leave to soak overnight. The next day, preheat the oven to 140°C/fan 120°C/275°F/gas mark 1. Grease a 20cm (8 inch) cake tin and line the base and sides with baking parchment.

2. Cream the butter and sugar in the bowl of a freestanding electric mixer (or you can use a handheld electric whisk and mixing bowl) until pale and fluffy. Beat in the eggs one at a time, mixing well after each addition. Sift the flour and spices over the creamed mixture, then gently fold it in until combined. Fold in the brandy-soaked fruit, sliced almonds, ground almonds and treacle.

3. Spoon the mixture into the prepared cake tin and spread evenly with the back of a spoon. Cut a small hole in the middle of a disc of double-thickness baking parchment (this will allow steam to escape while the cake is baking). Cover the top of the cake with the paper and bake on the lowest shelf of the oven for 3½–4 hours until a skewer inserted through the hole in the centre of the parchment paper comes out clean.

4. Remove from the oven and leave the cake to cool in the tin for 30 minutes before transferring to a wire rack to finish cooling. When the cake is cold, turn it upside down and make small holes in the base with a skewer. Sprinkle the 2 tbsp of brandy over the cake.

5. Double wrap the cake with parchment paper and place in an airtight container for up to three months, feeding it with more brandy every month if you wish.

To decorate:

825g (1lb 13oz) marzipan

825g (1lb 13oz) white fondant icing

Bottle-green fondant icing

Red fondant icing

2 tbsp apricot glaze

Red edible glitter

Edible pearl dust

TO DECORATE:

1. Gently melt the apricot glaze and brush over the whole cake. Lightly knead the marzipan until softened. Dust your work surface with icing sugar, and roll out the marzipan to a thickness of 5mm (¼ inch) to cover the entire cake, smoothing the sides using a cake smoother to get a perfect finish. Trim off any excess.

2. Gently brush the marzipan with water and then repeat the above process for the white fondant icing. Use a smoother to smooth the sides and top of the cake after you have trimmed off the excess.

3. When you have covered your cake with icing, roll out some bottle-green fondant icing, and using a holly leaf cutter, cut out enough holly leaves to make a holly wreath design. Put these to one side. Roll small balls of red fondant icing in your hands to resemble berries. Brush the fondant berries with some red edible glitter.

4. Using a little water, place your holly leaves and berries on top of the cake to resemble a Christmas wreath. Dust the holly leaves with a little edible pearl dust.

MINCE PIES

These traditional mince pies are a perfect Christmas treat.

(MAKES 10–12)

INGREDIENTS

50g (2oz) butter, cubed,
  plus extra for greasing
50g (2oz) lard or vegetable
  shortening, cubed
225g (8oz) plain flour
1 egg, beaten

For the egg wash:
1 egg
Few drops of milk

1 x jar shop-bought or homemade
  mincemeat (see page 188)

Amy's Tip
You can have fun making shapes
such as stars and Christmas
trees to top your mince pies.

METHOD

1. Preheat the oven to 200°C/fan 180°C/400°F/gas mark 6.
2. To make the pastry, sift the flour into a bowl, and using the tips of your fingers rub in the butter and lard (lifting your hands well above the bowl to incorporate as much air as possible) until the mixture resembles breadcrumbs (you can do this by hand or with an electric mixer or food processor). Add the beaten egg and use a knife to continue to mix until a dough forms, finishing with your hands. Knead lightly into a flat disc, then wrap in cling film and chill for 30 minutes.
3. Lightly flour your work surface. Roll half of the chilled dough out thinly and cut it into rounds using a fluted pastry cutter slightly larger than the holes of your tart tin, gathering and using any scraps of pastry.
4. Fit the rounds into a greased 12-hole tart tin. Spoon the mincemeat into the cases to the level of the edge of the pastry. Using the other half of dough roll out and cut lids using a slightly smaller fluted pastry cutter.
5. Dampen the edges of the lids with water and press them lightly into position, sealing the edges. Brush each one with the egg wash (to make an egg wash, whisk the egg with a few drops of milk), making a small hole with a sharp knife in the top of each pie to allow steam to escape during cooking. Serve warm, lightly dusted with icing sugar.

MINCEMEAT

Easy to make, a jar of homemade mincemeat is a lovely gift and an essential at Christmas for your homemade mince pies (I like to add glacé cherries to mine!).

INGREDIENTS

110g (4oz) shredded suet
225g (8oz) Bramley apples,
  cored and chopped small
175g (6oz) raisins
110g (4oz) currants
110g (4oz) sultanas
175g (6oz) soft dark brown sugar
250g (9oz) almonds, chopped
110g (4oz) mixed candied
  peel, chopped
75g (3oz) glacé cherries, chopped
2 tsp ground mixed spice
2 tsp ground cinnamon
1 tsp freshly grated nutmeg
Grated zest and juice of 1 lemon
Grated zest and juice of 1 orange
3 tbsp brandy (optional)

METHOD

1. Sterilise the jars. First wash the jars in soapy water and rinse in clear water. Place the jars upside down on a baking tray in the oven preheated to 180°C/fan 160°C/350°F/gas mark 4 for 5 minutes until dry (or you can carefully swill the washed jars with boiled water).

2. In a large mixing bowl, combine the ingredients, except for the brandy (if used), mixing them together thoroughly.

3. Cover the bowl with a clean cloth and leave the mixture in a cool place overnight, so that the flavours can develop. The next day, preheat the oven to 120°C/fan 100°C/225°F/gas mark 1. Transfer the mixture into an ovenproof dish. Cover loosely with foil and place in the oven for 3 hours.

4. Remove from the oven. As it cools stir occasionally. When the mincemeat is completely cold, stir in the brandy, if using.

5. Spoon the mincemeat into the sterilised jars. Seal immediately and store in a cool place until needed.

RED VELVET
ANGEL CUPCAKES

These beautiful cupcakes look like angels floating on clouds.

(MAKES 12)

INGREDIENTS

For the angel cupcakes:
200g (7oz) plain flour
1 tsp baking powder
1 tbsp cocoa powder
100g (3½oz) butter
175g (6oz) caster sugar
1 egg, beaten
2 tsp red paste food colouring
25g (1oz) dark chocolate, melted
1 tsp white wine vinegar
1 tsp vanilla extract
120ml (4fl.oz) buttermilk
2 tbsp vegetable oil

For the cream cheese frosting:
75g (3oz) butter
225g (8oz) cream cheese
175g (6oz) icing sugar, sifted

For decorating:
White fondant icing
Small amount of mincemeat or jam
Angel mould
Edible metallic gold paint
Fine decorating brush

METHOD

1. Dust your work surface with icing sugar and lightly knead your fondant icing until softened slightly. Roll out the fondant icing quite thinly. Using a round cutter that fits your cupcakes, cut out discs of fondant icing. Make 12 and set them aside to dry.

2. To make the angels, push a small amount of white fondant icing into the mould. When you have made 12 angels, use a decorating brush to paint them with edible gold paint for the finishing touch. Leave these to dry before decorating the cakes.

3. Preheat the oven to 180°C/fan 160°C/350°F/gas mark 4 and line a 12-hole muffin tin with gold foil muffin cases.

4. Sift together the flour, baking powder and cocoa powder into a mixing bowl.

5. Melt the dark chocolate in a heatproof bowl over a pan of simmering water.

6. Beat together the butter and sugar in the bowl of a free-standing electric mixer (or you can use a handheld electric whisk and mixing bowl) until light and fluffy. Gradually beat in the egg and slowly mix in the food colouring. Add the melted chocolate, vanilla extract, oil and vinegar on a low speed.

7. Gently fold in half of the sifted dry ingredients with a large metal spoon followed by half of the buttermilk. Repeat this process with the remaining dry ingredients and buttermilk.

8. Divide the mixture evenly between the cases. Bake in the preheated oven for 20–25 minutes until well risen and a skewer inserted into one of the cakes comes out clean. Remove from the oven and allow to cool in the tin for 10 minutes, then turn out onto a wire rack.

9. While your cakes are cooling, make the cream cheese frosting. Beat the butter and cream cheese together in the bowl of a free-standing electric mixer (or you can use a handheld electric whisk and mixing bowl). On a low speed, add the icing sugar in two additions until soft and creamy.

10. When your cupcakes are cool, you can begin to ice and decorate them. Spread a little mincemeat or jam onto each cake and place a fondant disc on top. This will help it to stick. Spoon the cream cheese frosting into a piping bag fitted with a star nozzle, and pipe a small swirl in the middle of each cupcake on top of the fondant disc. When you have done this with all your cupcakes, decorate them by placing your angels on top of the 'clouds' of cream cheese frosting.

CHRISTMAS BAKED ALASKA

A show-stopping retro classic that will impress your guests this Christmas.
You can use shop-bought ice cream, but for best results make your own.

(SERVES 8–10)

INGREDIENTS

For the vanilla ice cream:
800ml (1½ pints) double cream
800ml (1½ pints) full fat milk
350g (12oz) icing sugar
4 tsp vanilla extract

For the sponge base:
110g (4oz) butter, plus extra
  for greasing
110g (4oz) caster sugar
110g (4oz) self-raising flour
2 eggs
1 tsp vanilla extract
5 tbsp of shop-bought or
  homemade mincemeat
  (page 188)

For the meringue:
4 egg whites
225g (8oz) caster sugar

You will need:
800ml (1½ pint) round heatproof
  pudding basin, lined with cling
  film
Ice cream maker

METHOD

1. First make the ice cream. Mix the cream and milk together in a mixing bowl. Whisk in the icing sugar until it is dissolved, then stir in the vanilla extract. Transfer the mixture into the frozen bowl of the ice cream maker and leave to churn for about 40 minutes, or until thickened and starting to freeze. You may need to halve the mixture and churn in two batches. Once thickened, spoon the ice cream into the pudding basin lined with cling film, pressing it down to get a smooth surface. Cover with cling film and place in the freezer.

2. Preheat the oven to 180°C/fan 160°C/350°F/gas mark 4.

3. Grease an 18cm (7 inch) cake tin, and line the base with baking parchment. (To do this, draw around the base of the tin onto the baking parchment and cut out).

4. Put the butter, caster sugar, eggs and vanilla extract into the bowl of a free-standing electric mixer (or you can use a handheld electric whisk and mixing bowl). Then sift in the flour, lifting your sieve quite high to incorporate air, and beat for 1–2 minutes until light and creamy. Stir in 2 tbsp of mincemeat.

5. Spoon the mixture into the prepared cake tin, and bake in the preheated oven for 20–25 minutes or until well risen and a skewer inserted into the middle comes out clean. Remove from the oven and leave to cool in the tin for 10 minutes. Transfer to a wire rack to cool completely. When cool spread the remaining mincemeat over the top, and place on a baking tray or ovenproof dish.

6. Before you prepare the meringue, preheat the oven to 220°C/fan 200°C/425°F/gas mark 7.

7. Place the egg whites in a clean dry bowl. Beat with

the whisk attachment of an electric mixer until soft peaks form. Gradually add caster sugar, beating well between each addition. Beat until mixture is thick and glossy.

8. Remove the ice cream from the freezer. Allow it to sit for about 5 minutes and then ease out the ice cream with the help of cling film and place it upside down on top of the sponge base.

9. Quickly spoon the meringue thickly and in peaks over the ice cream, spreading it down to the base and covering the edge. Place immediately in the centre of the hot oven for 3–4 minutes or until the meringue is set and pale gold in colour. Remove your 'mountain' from the oven. Carefully transfer to a serving plate and serve immediately.

CANDY CANE BISCUITS

These minty candy cane biscuits are fun to make and a perfect stocking filler.

(MAKES 10)

INGREDIENTS

225g (8oz) plain flour
150g (5oz) butter
50g (2oz) caster sugar
1 egg, beaten
Red food colouring (gel/paste
 is best)
1 tsp peppermint extract

METHOD

1. Preheat the oven to 180°C/fan 160°C/350°F/gas mark 4 and line some baking trays with baking parchment. Each tray will fit 3–4 biscuits.

2. Sift the flour into a mixing bowl and using the tips of your fingers, rub in the butter until the texture is like breadcrumbs (you can do this by hand or with an electric mixer or food processor). Now add the sugar and the egg and, using a knife, continue to mix until it forms a soft dough. Flour your work surface, turn the dough out and knead into a ball.

3. Separate the dough into two halves. To one half add 1 tsp of peppermint extract. To the other half, add a little red food colouring using the tip of a cocktail stick and knead it into the dough until you get a bright red colour. Add more colouring if needed.

4. Roll out a tablespoon-size of dough of each colour into a long sausage shape, about 1cm (½ inch) thick. Do this with both colours. Lay both colours side by side and gently wrap each colour around the other. Curve one end of the straight candy cane biscuit. Lift the biscuits with a palette knife, place on the lined baking trays and trim each end. Repeat this process with the remaining dough.

5. Place in the oven for 10 minutes. Do not let the biscuits brown.

Merry Christmas

SNOWFLAKE BISCUITS

These gingerbread snowflakes make the perfect gift at Christmas.

(MAKES 20)

INGREDIENTS

110g (4oz) of butter
75g (3oz) light soft brown sugar
1 egg
2½ tbsp golden syrup
350g (12oz) plain flour
1 tsp bicarbonate soda
3 tsp ground ginger

For the royal icing:
500g (1lb 2oz) icing sugar
3 egg whites
2 tsp lemon juice
Small piping bag

You will need:
Snowflake cutter

METHOD

1. Preheat the oven to 180°C/fan 160°C/350°F/gas mark 4.
2. Cream the butter and the sugar until light and fluffy. Add the egg and beat well.
3. Sift the dry ingredients and add them gradually to the mixture. Add the syrup, mix well and then knead lightly.
4. Roll out the dough onto baking parchment to 5mm (¼ inch) thickness. Cut out dough using a snowflake-shaped cutter. Line some baking trays with baking parchment and lift the snowflakes using a palette knife and place onto the lined sheets.
5. Bake in the preheated oven for 10 minutes, then cool on a wire rack.
6. Prepare the royal icing. Whisk the egg white until frothy. Gradually add the icing sugar, beating in well after each addition. Beat in lemon juice until smooth.
7. Spoon the royal icing into a piping bag, snip the top and ice your biscuits so they resemble snowflakes.

SALTED CARAMEL PEANUT BUTTER CUPS

These bitesized treats are perfect to serve after dinner or to give as a gift at Christmas. They are one of my favourites!

(MAKES 35)

INGREDIENTS

For the base:
200g (7oz) smooth peanut butter
200g (7oz) icing sugar
50g (2oz) butter
Gold petit four cases

For the salted caramel:
100g (3½oz) light muscovado sugar
4 tbsp golden syrup
100g (3½oz) butter
4 tbsp double cream
1 tsp salt

For the topping:
100g (3½oz) milk chocolate
100g (3½oz) high quality dark
  chocolate (70% cocoa solids)
Edible gold leaf

METHOD

1. First, make the salted caramel sauce. Melt the sugar, syrup, salt and butter in a small saucepan and bring slowly to the boil. Reduce the heat and simmer for 3 minutes or so until thick. Stir in the cream, remove from the heat and set aside to cool and thicken.

2. To make the peanut butter base, place the icing sugar, butter and peanut butter in a mixing bowl and mix using an electric mixer. Beat until it forms a paste. Line a mini muffin tin with gold petit four cases. Spoon 1 tsp of the peanut butter mixture into each gold case and press it down with your fingers.

3. When the salted caramel sauce has cooled and thickened, spoon a thin layer into each case on top of the peanut butter mixture. Put in the fridge for 15 minutes until the caramel has set a little.

4. While they are chilling, make the chocolate topping. In a heatproof bowl over a pan of simmering water, melt together the milk and dark chocolate and leave to cool. Take the peanut butter cups out of the fridge when the caramel has set. Spoon 1 tsp of the cooled melted chocolate into each case.

5. Chill for 30 minutes so they can set, then adorn with edible gold leaf for the finishing touch before serving.

RED VELVET CUPCAKE ICE CREAM

My unique and delicious recipe combines my two favourite things – red velvet cupcakes and homemade ice cream.

(SERVES 4–6)

INGREDIENTS

For the ice cream:

300ml (10fl.oz/½ pint) double cream
300ml (10fl.oz/½ pint) full fat milk
110g (4oz) icing sugar
2 tsp vanilla extract

For the red velvet cupcakes:

100g (3½oz) plain flour
½ tsp baking powder
½ tbsp cocoa powder
50g (2oz) butter
75g (3oz) caster sugar
1 egg, beaten
1 tsp red food colouring
  (gel/paste is best)
10g (½oz) melted dark chocolate
½ tsp white wine vinegar
½ tsp vanilla extract
60ml (2fl.oz) buttermilk
1 tbsp vegetable oil

For the cream cheese frosting:

50g (2oz) butter,
  at room temperature
175g (6oz) cream cheese
110g (4oz) icing sugar

METHOD

1. First make your cupcakes. Preheat the oven to 180°C/fan 160°C/350°F/gas mark 4 and line a muffin tin with 6 paper cupcake or muffin cases.

2. Melt the dark chocolate in a heatproof bowl over a pan of simmering water.

3. Sift together the flour, baking powder and cocoa powder into a mixing bowl.

4. Beat together the butter and sugar in the bowl of a free-standing electric mixer (or you can use a handheld electric whisk and mixing bowl) until light and fluffy. Gradually beat in the egg and slowly mix in the food colouring. Now add the melted chocolate, vanilla extract, oil and vinegar on a low speed. In two halves fold in the dry ingredients followed by the buttermilk.

5. Divide the mixture between the 6 muffin cases and bake in a preheated oven for 20–25 minutes until well risen and a skewer inserted comes out clean. Remove from the oven and allow to cool on a wire rack.

6. Now make your cream cheese frosting while the cakes are cooling. This will go in the ice cream as well. Beat the butter until very soft and smooth. Add the cream cheese and beat for 2 minutes.

7. Sift the icing sugar and gradually add it on a low speed until incorporated, then beat it on a higher speed until the icing is smooth. Put half of the icing into a container and place in the freezer. Put the other half in the fridge.

8. Now make the ice cream. Mix the cream and milk together in a mixing bowl. Whisk in the icing sugar until it is dissolved then stir in the vanilla extract.

9. Transfer the mixture into the frozen bowl of the ice cream maker and leave it to churn for about 40 minutes, until thickened and starting to freeze.

10. Once thickened, take the frozen cream cheese frosting out of the freezer and cut into small pieces. Fold the pieces of frozen frosting and the smooth, unfrozen refrigerated frosting into the churned ice cream. Remove the red velvet cupcakes from the cases and break them up into small pieces. Gently fold these into the ice cream.

11. Transfer the churned ice cream to a plastic container, cover with a lid and freeze for 4–6 hours or overnight until completely frozen.

NEW YEAR'S EVE CUPCAKE CLOCK

Count down to the New Year with this cupcake clock to enjoy at midnight with friends and family.

(MAKES 12)

INGREDIENTS

For the chocolate cupcakes:
175g (6oz) butter
175g (6oz) caster sugar
150g (5oz) self-raising flour
25g (1oz) cocoa powder
3 eggs

For the vanilla buttercream:
225g (8oz) butter
450g (1lb) icing sugar
2–3 tbsp milk
1 tsp vanilla extract

For decorating:
White fondant icing
200g dark chocolate
Small piping bag
Large silver cake board
  (on which to display
  your cakes to resemble
  a clock)

METHOD

1. Preheat the oven to 180°C/fan 160°C/350°F/gas mark 4 and line a 12-hole muffin tin with silver foil muffin cases.

2. Put the butter, caster sugar and eggs into the bowl of a free-standing electric mixer (or you can use a handheld electric whisk and mixing bowl). Then sift in the flour and cocoa powder, lifting your sieve quite high to incorporate air, and beat for 1–2 minutes until light and creamy. Divide the mixture evenly between the muffin cases.

3. Bake in the preheated oven for 20–25 minutes until well risen and a skewer inserted into one of the cakes comes out clean. Remove from the oven and leave to cool in the tin for 10 minutes, then remove from the tin and transfer to a wire rack to cool completely.

4. Meanwhile, prepare the buttercream. Put the butter in a bowl of a free-standing electric mixer (or you can use a handheld electric whisk and mixing bowl) and beat well until soft and creamy. Sift the icing sugar and add to the creamed butter in two additions, mixing on a slow speed.

5. Add the vanilla extract and milk and beat again until smooth.

6. Spoon the buttercream into a piping bag fitted with a star nozzle and swirl it on top of the cupcakes.

7. Dust the worktop with icing sugar and roll out the fondant icing. Cut into 12 round discs using a round cutter to fit each cupcake.

8. Break the chocolate into small pieces and put it in a heatproof bowl. Half fill a pan with water and bring to the boil, then turn down so the water is simmering. Put the bowl of chocolate onto the pan making sure the water does not touch the bottom of the bowl. Wait for the chocolate to melt completely and stir with a wooden spoon to distribute the heat evenly. When the chocolate is melted, turn off the heat and using oven gloves, lift the bowl of chocolate off the pan.

9. Once the chocolate is cooled, snip the tip of the small piping bag and using a spatula or spoon fill the bag with the melted chocolate. Pipe Roman numerals 1–12 (I – XII) on each disc and pipe clock hands onto the cake board. When the chocolate has dried place the discs onto the swirled cupcakes and arrange on the cake board in order from 1–12 (I–XII) in a clockwise direction.

Happy New Year!

Valentine's Day

Show your appreciation for those you love by baking them some heart-shaped creations.

Heart-Shaped Ombré Ruffle Cake   210

Mini Red Velvet Heart Cakes   213

Lollipop Biscuits   216

HEART-SHAPED OMBRÉ RUFFLE CAKE

This impressive celebration cake is perfect to share on any occasion.

(SERVES 8–10)

INGREDIENTS

For the red velvet layer:
200g (7oz) plain flour
100g (3½oz) butter
175g (6oz) caster sugar
1 tbsp cocoa powder
1 tsp baking powder
1 egg
2 tsp red food colouring
  (gel/paste is best)
25g (1oz) melted dark chocolate
1 tsp white wine vinegar
1 tsp vanilla extract
125ml (4fl.oz) buttermilk
2 tbsp vegetable oil

For the vanilla cake layers:
525g (1lb 3oz) self-raising flour
525g (1lb 3oz) butter
525g (1lb 3oz) caster sugar
3 tsp vanilla extract
9 eggs
Pink food colouring (gel/paste
  is best)

METHOD

1. First, make the red velvet layer for the four-layered cake. Preheat the oven to 180°C/fan 160°C/350°F/gas mark 4. Melt the chocolate in a bowl over a pan of simmering water. Sift together the flour, baking powder and cocoa powder in a bowl. Beat the butter and sugar together in the bowl of a free-standing electric mixer (or you can use a handheld electric whisk and mixing bowl) until pale and fluffy. Slowly beat in the egg and mix in the food colouring. Slowly beat in the melted chocolate, vinegar, oil and vanilla extract. Gently fold in the dry ingredients and buttermilk in two stages. Grease one of your heart-shaped tins and pour the mixture into it. Bake for 25–30 minutes in a preheated oven until a skewer inserted in the middle comes out clean. Leave to cool on a wire rack.

2. Now make the vanilla cake for the other three layers. Sift the flour and baking powder into a bowl. Cream the butter and sugar in the bowl of a free-standing electric mixer (or you can use a handheld electric whisk and mixing bowl) until pale and fluffy. Add the vanilla extract and mix well. Add the eggs one at a time, beating well between each addition. Slowly add the sifted dry ingredients and beat starting on a low speed until combined. Divide the mixture between three large bowls. Add different amounts of pink food colouring into each bowl and mix together so you have three different shades of pink. Pour each into a separate cake tin. Bake the cakes in the oven for 25–30 minutes until a skewer inserted in the middle comes out clean. Leave to cool on a wire rack before icing.

3. While your cakes are cooling, make the Swiss

For the Swiss meringue frosting:
350g (12oz) caster sugar
10 egg whites
900g (2lbs) butter
3 tsp vanilla extract
Pinch of salt

You will need:
Heart-shaped tins (I use shallow
  tins of 9 inches x 1¼ inches/
  20 x 3cm)
Piping bag and rose petal nozzle

Amy's Tip

You may want to practise piping ruffles on a plate first before you pipe onto your cake.

meringue frosting to ice your cake. Place a heatproof bowl on top of a pan of simmering water. Whisk the egg whites and sugar in a bowl until the sugar has dissolved. Remove from the heat and using the whisk attachment of an electric mixer, whip the mixture until it is thick, glossy and cool. Add the softened chunks of butter to the frosting and continue to mix until fully combined and smooth. Add the vanilla extract and salt and mix well.

4. When your cakes are completely cool, begin to sandwich them together with the frosting in between each layer. Do this so the red velvet cake layer is at the bottom and the lightest shade of pink tinted vanilla cake is at the top. Make sure they are lined up. Using the frosting, cover your four-layered cake with a thin smooth layer all over.

5. Once you have done this, fill a piping bag fitted with a rose petal nozzle with the remaining frosting. Start piping the icing onto your cake the whole way around the sides by starting at the bottom of your cake with the thinner end of the nozzle pointing towards you. Begin to squeeze the icing out at the same time as moving it upwards and in a wave motion from side to side. It should look like a frill. Continue this around the cake until covered. Do the same on the top of the cake but in a heart shape. Leave a heart in the middle of the top of the cake like I have, to dust over with some gold edible glitter.

MINI RED VELVET HEART CAKES

Give these heart-shaped cakes as a gift on Valentine's Day. You'll be loved.

(MAKES 12)

INGREDIENTS

200g (7oz) plain flour

1 tsp baking powder

1 tbsp cocoa powder

100g (3½oz) butter

175g (6oz) caster sugar

1 egg, beaten

2 tsp red food colouring
   (gel/paste is best)

25g (1oz) dark chocolate, melted

1 tsp white wine vinegar

1 tsp vanilla extract

125ml (4fl.oz) buttermilk

2 tbsp vegetable oil

For the cream cheese frosting:

75g (3oz) butter

225g (8oz) cream cheese

175g (6oz) icing sugar

You will need:

Heart-shaped muffin tin (or you can
   use a standard square cake tin and
   cut out cakes with a heart-shaped
   cutter)

METHOD

1. Preheat the oven to 180°C/fan 160°C/350°F/gas mark 4 and lightly grease a 12-hole heart-shaped muffin tin.

2. Sift together the flour, baking powder and cocoa powder into a mixing bowl.

3. Melt the dark chocolate by placing in a mixing bowl. Add water into a saucepan and heat on a medium heat. Once the water is hot, place the mixing bowl over the saucepan and leave the chocolate to melt.

4. Beat together the butter and sugar in the bowl of a free-standing electric mixer (or you can use a handheld electric whisk and mixing bowl) until light and fluffy. Gradually beat in the beaten egg and slowly mix in the food colouring. Now add the melted chocolate, vanilla extract, buttermilk, oil and vinegar. Gently fold in half the sifted dry ingredients with a large metal spoon followed by half of the buttermilk. Repeat this process with the remaining dry ingredients and buttermilk.

5. Divide the mixture between the lightly greased heart-shaped muffin tin. Bake in the preheated oven for 20–25 minutes until well risen and a skewer inserted into one of the cakes comes out clean. Remove from the oven and allow to cool in the tin for 10 minutes. Transfer to a wire rack to cool completely. If you don't have a heart-shaped muffin tin, use a square cake tin. When the cake is cooled, cut using a heart-shaped cutter into individual heart-shaped cakes.

6. While your cakes are cooling down, make the cream cheese frosting. Beat the butter in a bowl of a free-standing electric mixer (or you can use a handheld electric whisk and mixing bowl) until very

My Valentine ♡

soft and smooth. Add the cream cheese and beat for 2 minutes. Sift the icing sugar and gradually add it until incorporated and the frosting is smooth and glossy.

7. With a sharp knife, slice off the bottoms of the individual cakes so they are level.

8. Ice your cakes with a small rounded knife or small palette knife until fully covered. To decorate, make some red fondant roses (page 110) and dust with red edible glitter.

LOLLIPOP BISCUITS

These lollipop biscuits are a fun gift for Valentine's Day.

(MAKES 10–15 DEPENDING ON THE SIZE OF YOUR HEART-SHAPED CUTTER)

INGREDIENTS

For the biscuits:

225g (8oz) plain flour

150g (5oz) butter

50g (2oz) caster sugar

1 egg, beaten

For the glacé icing:

500g (1lb 2oz) icing sugar

5–6 tbsp water

Few drops rosewater

Pink food colouring (gel/paste
  is best)

Red food colouring (gel/paste
  is best)

You will need:

20cm (8 inch) lollipop sticks

Heart-shaped cutter

Cocktail sticks

Fondant rose decorations
  (see page 110)

METHOD

1. Preheat the oven to 180°C/fan 160°C/350°F/gas mark 4 and lightly grease two baking trays.

2. Sift the flour into a mixing bowl and using the tips of your fingers rub in the butter until the texture is like breadcrumbs. (You can do this by hand or with an electric mixer or food processor). Add the sugar and the egg and mix using a knife until it forms a soft dough. Flour your work surface. Turn the dough out and knead into a ball. Wrap in cling film and chill for 30 minutes.

3. Roll out the dough to a thickness of 5mm (¼ inch) and cut out using a heart-shaped cutter.

4. Lift the biscuits using a palette knife and place onto the baking trays. Carefully push a lollipop stick into the centre of each biscuit. Cover the end of the stick that has been pushed into the dough with a little more dough. Bake for 10 minutes in the preheated oven until a pale golden colour and the edges are browning just slightly. Remove from the oven, then cool on a wire rack.

5. To make the glacé icing, sift the icing sugar into a bowl and mix in a tablespoon of water at a time until you have a runny icing. Mix in the rosewater.

6. Divide icing into separate bowls and mix in your food colourings using the tip of a cocktail stick. Turn the baked biscuits over so there is a flat surface for you to ice. Make a small snip to the tip of a piping bag and turn the top half of the piping bag inside out. Place the piping bag in a tall glass or jug and pour in the icing. Pipe a steady outline around each biscuit. Snip the tip of the piping bag again to make a slightly larger hole, and pipe and fill in (flood) the centres of the biscuits. Use a cocktail stick to carefully spread and fill in any gaps up to the piped outline.

7. Before they have set, decorate with fondant decorations such as roses, like I have.

Lollipop biscuits

Ingredients-
225g / 8oz plain flour
140g / 5oz butter
55g / 2oz caster sugar
lollipop sticks

Method-
Preheat the oven to
170°C / 350°F / Gas 4,
grease the tin or, and
___ing sheet

Sift the flour
___ mixing bowl
___ the butter un___
___xture is like ___
Add the sugar ___
continue to mix
the ingredients to___
together as a lar___
dough.
___oll out to 1cm (
___nd cut out ___

CONVERSION TABLES

Mark 1	275°F	140°C
2	300	150
3	325	170
4	350	180
5	375	190
6	400	200
7	425	220
8	450	230
9	475	240

If using a fan oven, reduce the temperature by 20°C

AMERICAN CUP CONVERSIONS

American	Imperial	Metric
1 cup flour	5oz	150g
1 cup caster/granulated sugar	8oz	225g
1 cup brown sugar	6oz	175g
1 cup butter/margarine/lard	8oz	225g
1 cup sultanas/raisins	7oz	200g
1 cup currants	5oz	150g
1 cup ground almonds	4oz	110g
1 cup golden syrup	12oz	350g
1 cup grated cheese	4oz	110g
1 stick butter	4oz	110g

MEASUREMENTS

⅛ inch	3mm
¼	5mm
½	1cm
¾	2
1	2.5
1¼	3
1½	4
1¾	4.5
2	5
2½	6
3	7.5
3½	9
4	10
5	13
5¼	13.5
6	15
6½	16
7	18
7½	19
8	20
9	23
9½	24
10	25.5
11	28
12	30

WEIGHTS

½oz	10g
¾	20
1	25
1½	40
2	50
2½	60
3	75
4	110
4½	125
5	150
6	175
7	200
8	225
9	250
10	275
12	350
1lb	450
1½	700
2	900
3	1.35kg

LIQUID MEASUREMENTS

Metric	Imperial
30ml	1fl.oz
60	2
100	3
125	4
150	5 (¼ pint)
190	6
250	8
300	10 (½ pint)
500	16
600	20 (1 pint)
1000 (1 litre)	1¾ pints

Metric	American
30ml	2 tablespoons
60	¼ cup
125	½ cup
190	¾ cup
250	1 cup
300	1¼ cup
500	2 cups
600	2½ cups
1000 (1 litre)	4 cups

AMY'S BAKING ESSENTIALS

You can add to your equipment over time, but your collection could include:

BAKING EQUIPMENT

Apron – for keeping you clean

Oven gloves – for hand protection

Free-standing electric mixer – for making cakes, buttercream and biscuit dough
I wouldn't be without my Kitchen Aid stand mixer. Although this is not essential, it is worth investing in, if you plan to do a lot of baking, but if you don't have a free-standing electric mixer, you can use a handheld electric whisk

Food processor – for making pastry and biscuit dough
This isn't essential, but it is a lot quicker than using your hands

Kitchen scales – for weighing out ingredients

Sieve – for getting any lumps out of flour and icing sugar, and for getting air into the mixture for a light and fluffy cake

Wooden spoons – for stirring hot jam, and fudge
This causes less damage to your saucepan

Measuring spoons – for measuring small quantities

Small and large whisks – for whisking eggs

Large rolling pin – for rolling out dough

Pastry brush – for glazing

Spatulas – for scraping the last of the mixture from the bowl as well as for gently folding mixtures together

Mixing bowls – for mixing ingredients
Stainless steel and ceramic mixing bowls are best

Pyrex mixing bowl – for melting chocolate and for cooking lemon curd

Wire racks – for cooling cakes and biscuits

Baking parchment – for lining tins and baking trays

Cling film – for covering dough for chilling and for covering bowls of icing to stop them drying out

Cake and muffin tins – there are lots of types available. I've listed the ones I use in this book below. Round, square and muffin tins are the most versatile

Round seamless cake tins 1 x 15cm (6 inch) and 1 x 20cm (8 inch) – for my two-tiered cake

Standard square cake tin 20cm (8 inch) x 20cm (8 inch) – for slab cake for my fondant fancies

2 x sandwich tins 20cm (8 inch) – for Grandma's Victoria sponge

Bundt tin – for ring-shaped cakes such as my spiced pumpkin bundt cake

Mini pudding tins – for my sticky toffee puddings

12-hole tartlet tins – for jam tarts and mince pies

Pie tin: 20cm (8 inch) round tin – for my apple, plum and blackberry pie

12-hole muffin tin – for cupcakes and butterfly cakes

Mini muffin tin – for my strawberries and cream cupcakes

Heart-shaped muffin tin – for my red velvet heart cakes

Baking trays – for baking biscuits

Paper muffin and cupcake cases – to line your muffin and cupcake tins and to bake and dress your cupcakes. I often use classic white muffin cases for my cupcakes, which make a larger cupcake than standard fairy cake cases

There are lots of cake decorating tools and accessories available, giving unlimited opportunities to get creative! Here are some of the ones I use in this book:

Large and small palette knives – for applying buttercream

Icing smoother – for achieving a really smooth finish on your Christmas cake

Piping bags and nozzles – for swirling buttercream onto cupcakes and decorating cakes and biscuits

Cocktail sticks – for tinting icings and for assembling my cupcake bouquet

Tea-strainer – for dusting cakes and your work surface with flour

Circular cutter – for making round biscuits and fondant discs for my strawberry basket cakes and my New Year cupcake clock

Fluted circular cutter – for jam tarts and mince pies

Small rolling pin – for rolling out ready-to-roll fondant icing

Acrylic cake pop stand – to hold cake pops to decorate

For some of the more elaborate decorations in this book, you will need:

Paint palette – for mixing the cake dust for my hand-painted Mother's Day biscuits
This is not an essential: you can use a plate

Fine paint brushes – for painting cake dust colouring onto my hand-painted Mother's Day biscuits

Dusting brushes – for brushing edible dust onto fondant decorations

Flower plunger cutter – for making tiny fondant flowers

Large and small butterfly-shaped cutters – for making fondant butterflies

Shaped cutters – for making hearts, stars, daisies, teapots, teacups and holly leaves

Daffodil cutter – for making fondant daffodils

Small bunny-shaped cutter – for making fondant bunnies

Leaf plunger cutter – for making fondant leaves

Assorted leaf-shaped cutters – for making autumn leaf biscuits

Angel-shaped mould – for making angel cupcake fondant decorations

Ball tool – for thinning the edges of handmade fondant roses and flowers

Lollipop sticks – for cake pops and my lollipop biscuits

Dipping fork – for dipping fondant fancies into icing

Selection of cellophane bags, pretty boxes and ribbon – for presenting your edible gifts and for selling at your cake sale

Large serrated knife – for layering my two-tiered celebration cake

Small knife

Grater – for finely zesting orange and lemon peels

Sugar thermometer – for checking the temperature of jam

Electric ice cream maker – for churning ice cream

Glass jars – for storing jam and chutney

Airtight tins –for keeping your bakes fresh. Don't put cakes into tins until they're completely cool

DIRECTORY

Baker & Maker
www.bakerandmaker.com
Stylish and unique new and vintage baking and cake supplies, party goods, craft and gifts from around the world.

Bombay Duck
www.bombayduck.com
Beautiful and individual gifts and accessories. Pretty vintage tea sets and cake stands.

Cake Craft World
www.cakecraftworld.co.uk
Suppliers of cake decorating equipment, sugar craft supplies and cake decorations such as edible glitter and cake dusts.

Eat My Flowers
www.eatmyflowers.co.uk
For hand-crystallised edible flowers.

Dunelm
www.dunelm-mill.com
Homeware and soft furnishings.

Hobbycraft
Visit www.hobbycraft.co.uk for your nearest stockist
For everything you need to get crafty, along with baking equipment such as cake tins, cake decorating equipment and cake stands.

Lakeland
www.lakeland.co.uk
For kitchen and baking equipment such as cupcake tins, cake decorations, storage containers etc., as well as cake stands to display cupcakes and cakes.

Loop the Loop
www.looptheloop.co.uk
A stylish collection of homeware with a vintage/industrial edge.
01873 812524

Magpie Miller
www.magpiemiller.co.uk
An online boutique that sources unique and individual homeware.

Mia fleur
http://www.miafleur.com
An online boutique selling a range of exquisite interiors products, partly designed and handmade by us in the UK.

Peach blossom
www.peachblossom.co.uk
Pretty and stylish party products.

QVC
www.qvcuk.com
Online bakeware and homeware.

Squires Kitchen
www.cakedecoratingstore.co.uk
Cake decorating supplies.

Steamer Trading
www.steamer.co.uk
Baking, tableware, electricals, and more.

The Sweet Hostess
www.thesweethostess.co.uk
Online party products, decorations, drinkware and sweet things.

For flowers:
2 Tulip
Clarks Lane, Epping, Essex, CM16 4NJ
01992 577320

For flowers and homeware:
Amy Louise Floral Design
www.amylouiseflorist.co.uk

Amy sourced her vintage wardrobe from:
Lucy in Disguise
www.lucyindisguiselondon.com
For exclusive vintage fashion.

Hair and make-up:
Louise Heywood of Artistic Licence Agency
www.artisticlicenceagency.com

Amy would like to thank Kitchen Aid for the loan
of the frosted pearl stand mixer featured in the
'Winter' chapter of *Amy's Baking Year*.
Visit www.kitchenaid.com for nearest stockists.

INDEX

A

Amy's Baking Essentials 222–3
Apple, Blackberry and Plum Pie 167
apple juice 161
apples:
    Apple, Blackberry and Plum Pie 167
    Chocolate Apples 147
    Toffee Apple Cupcakes 151
    Toffee Apple Jam 150
'As Pretty as a Picture' Mother's Day Biscuits 32
Auntie Lynn's Fudge 82
Autumn Chutney 162
Autumn Leaf Biscuits 158

B

Baked Alaska 193
baking essentials 222–3
berries:
    Apple, Blackberry and Plum Pie 167
    Blackberry Cheesecake Jars 94
    Blackberry Cordial 91
    Blackberry Drizzle Muffins 93
    Blackberry Jam 88
    Fresh Strawberry Ice Cream 66
    Mini Raspberry, Lemon and Chocolate Éclairs 115
    Raspberry Iced Bunny Biscuits 54
    Raspberry Iced Tea 112
    Strawberry Basket Cakes 98
    Strawberry Jam 74
    White Chocolate, Raspberry and Rose Petal Cake 25
Birthday Cupcakes 132
biscuits:
    Autumn Leaf Biscuits 158
    Candy Cane Biscuits 196
    Easter Bonnet Biscuits 51
    Fabergé Easter Egg Biscuits 42
    High Tea Biscuits 126
    Lollipop Biscuits 216

    Mother's Day Biscuits 32
    'As Pretty as a Picture' Mother's Day Biscuits 32
    Raspberry Iced Bunny Biscuits 54
    Shirt and Tie Biscuits 136
    Snowflake Biscuits 198
    Stained Glass Window Biscuits 180
blackberries:
    Apple, Blackberry and Plum Pie 167
    Blackberry Cheesecake Jars 94
    Blackberry Cordial 91
    Blackberry Drizzle Muffins 93
    Blackberry Jam 88
Blackberry Cheesecake Jars 94
Blackberry Cordial 91
Blackberry Drizzle Muffins 93
Blackberry Jam 88
Bonfire Night-themed recipes:
    Apple, Blackberry and Plum Pie 167
    Autumn Chutney 162
    Autumn Leaf Biscuits 158
    Hot Cocoa with Homemade Marshmallows 168
    Mulled Cider 161
    Sticky Toffee Puddings 164
    Toffee Apple Cupcakes 151
Bread 86

C

Cake Pops 123
cakes:
    Cake Pops 123
    Chocolate Celebration Cake 138
    Christmas Cake 182
    Heart-shaped Ombré Ruffle Cake 210
    Lemon Layer Easter Cake 47
    Mini Red Velvet Heart Cakes 213
    My Mum's Butterfly Cakes 69
    Spiced Pumpkin Bundt Cake 154
    Strawberry Basket Cakes 98
    Two-tiered Celebration Cake 104
    White Chocolate, Raspberry and Rose Petal

Cake 25
  see also celebration cakes
Candy Cane Biscuits 196
caramel sauce 201
caramelised onion 101
celebration cakes:
  Chocolate Celebration Cake 138
  Heart-Shaped Ombré Ruffle Cake 210
  Two-Tiered Celebration Cake 104
  see also cakes
Cheese Scones 97
  see also Scones (sweet)
chocolate:
  Chocolate Apples 147
  Chocolate Celebration Cake 138
  Chocolate Easter Nest Cupcakes 48
  Chocolate Orange Whoopie Pies 148
  Mini Raspberry, Lemon and Chocolate Éclairs 115
  Mint Chocolate Chip Ice Cream 64
  White Chocolate Chip Cookies 79
  White Chocolate, Raspberry and Rose Petal
    Cake 25
Chocolate Apples 147
Chocolate Celebration Cake 138
Chocolate Easter Nest Cupcakes 48
Chocolate Orange Whoopie Pies 148
chopped nuts 79, 82, 147, 164
choux pastry 115
Christmas Baked Alaska 193
Christmas Cake 182
Christmas-themed recipes:
  Candy Cane Biscuits 196
  Christmas Baked Alaska 193
  Christmas Cake 182
  as gifts 173, 174–5
  Gingerbread House 176
  Mince Pies 185
  Mincemeat 188
  New Year's Eve Cupcake Clock 205
  Red Velvet Angel Cupcakes 190
  Red Velvet Cupcake Ice Cream 202

  Salted Caramel Peanut Butter Cups 201
  Snowflake Biscuits 198
  Stained Glass Window Biscuits 180
chutney 162
cider, mulled 161
Cinnamon Sugar Doughnuts 144
coconut 80
conversion tables 221
cordial 85
Crystallised Rose Petals and Flowers 24
Cupcake Bouquet 16
cupcakes:
  Birthday Cupcakes 132
  Chocolate Easter Nest Cupcakes 48
  Cupcake Bouquet 16
  Lemon Daffodil Cupcakes 40
  Mini Strawberries and Cream Cupcakes 124
  Mother's Day Cupcakes 18
  New Year's Eve Cupcake Clock 205
  Red Velvet Angel Cupcakes 190
  Red Velvet Cupcake Ice Cream 202
  Rosy Teacup Cupcakes 108
  Toffee Apple Cupcakes 151

D
directory of resources 225–6
doughnuts 144
drinks:
  Blackberry Cordial 91
  equipment 225
  Homemade Lemonade 72
  Hot Cocoa with Homemade Marshmallows 168
  Mulled Cider 161
  Raspberry Iced Tea 112
duck eggs, as decorative ornaments 56

E
Easter Bonnet Biscuits 51
Easter-themed recipes:
  Chocolate Easter Nest Cupcakes 48
  duck eggs, as decorative ornaments 56

Easter Bonnet Biscuits 51
Fabergé Easter Egg Biscuits 42
Fondant Daffodils 38
Lemon Daffodil Cupcakes 40
Lemon Layer Easter Cake 47
Pastel Easter Eggs 56
Raspberry Iced Bunny Biscuits 54
edible flowers and leaves:
    Crystallised Rose Petals and Flowers 24
    Fresh Floral Ice Cubes 114
    Mint Chocolate Chip Ice Cream 65
    Rose Petal Jam 107
    where to buy 225
    White Chocolate, Raspberry and Rose Petal
        Cake 25–7
English Madeleines 120
equipment 222–3

F
Fabergé Easter Egg Biscuits 42
Father's Day-themed recipes:
    Chocolate Celebration Cake 138
    Shirt and Tie Biscuits 136
Fondant Daffodils 38
Fondant Fancies 118
Fondant Roses 110
French Macarons 29
Fresh Floral Ice Cubes 114
Fresh Strawberry Ice Cream 66
fruit-containing recipes:
    Autumn Chutney 162
    Blackberry Cheesecake Jars 94
    Blackberry Cordial 91
    Blackberry Drizzle Muffins 93
    Blackberry Jam 88
    Chocolate Apples 147
    Chocolate Orange Whoopie Pies 148
    Fresh Strawberry Ice Cream 66
    Homemade Lemonade 72
    Jam Tarts 76
    Lemon Curd 44

Lemon Layer Easter Cake 47
Mince Pies 185
Mincemeat 188
Mini Raspberry, Lemon and Chocolate Éclairs
    115
Mulled Cider 161
Raspberry Iced Bunny Biscuits 54
Raspberry Iced Tea 112
Rose Petal Jam 107
Strawberry Basket Cakes 98
Strawberry Jam 74
Toffee Apple Cupcakes 151
Toffee Apple Jam 150
White Chocolate, Raspberry and Rose Petal
    Cake 25

G
gift ideas 29, 48, 51, 80, 123, 136, 162, 173, 174, 188,
    198, 201, 213, 216
    supplies for 223, 225
Gingerbread House 176
Grandad's Coconut Ice 80
Grandma's Victoria Sponge 62

H
Halloween-themed recipes:
    Cinnamon Sugar Doughnuts 144
    Chocolate Apples 147
    Chocolate Orange Whoopie Pies 148
    Spiced Pumpkin Bundt Cake 154
    Toffee Apple Cupcakes 151
    Toffee Apple Jam 150
Handmade Fondant Decorations 22
Heart-shaped Ombré Ruffle Cake 210
High Tea Biscuits 126
homemade ice cream
    equipment for 223
    shop-bought versus 193
    see also ice cream
Homemade Lemonade 72
Hot Cocoa with Homemade Marshmallows 168

I

ice cream:
    Christmas Baked Alaska 193
    Fresh Strawberry Ice Cream 66
    homemade, equipment for 223
    Mint Chocolate Chip Ice Cream 65
    Red Velvet Cupcake Ice Cream 202

J

Jam Tarts 76
jams:
    Blackberry Jam 88
    Rose Petal Jam 107
    Strawberry Jam 74
    Toffee Apple Jam 150

K

kitchen equipment 222–3

L

leaf gelatine 168
Lemon Curd 44
Lemon Daffodil Cupcakes 40
Lemon Layer Easter Cake 47
lemons:
    Homemade Lemonade 72
    Lemon Curd 44
    Lemon Daffodil Cupcakes 40
    Lemon Layer Easter Cake 47
    Mini Raspberry, Lemon and Chocolate Éclairs 115
Lollipop Biscuits 216

M

madeleines 120
marshmallows 51, 168
measurement tables 221
Mince Pies 185
Mincemeat 188
Mini Pavlovas 128
Mini Raspberry, Lemon and Chocolate Éclairs 115

Mini Red Velvet Heart Cakes 213
Mini Strawberries and Cream Cupcakes 124
Mint Chocolate Chip Ice Cream 64
Mother's Day-themed recipes:
    'As Pretty as a Picture' Mother's Day Biscuits 32
    Mother's Day Cupcakes 18
Mother's Day Biscuits 32
Mother's Day Cupcakes 18
muffins 93
Mulled Cider 161
My Mum's Butterfly Cakes 69

N

New Year's Eve Cupcake Clock 205
nuts 79, 82, 147, 164

P

pansy petals:
    Crystallised Rose Petals and Flowers 24
    where to buy 225
    see also edible flowers and leaves
Pastel Easter Eggs 56
pavlovas 128
peanut butter 201
picnic-themed recipes:
    Blackberry Cordial 91
    Blackberry Cheesecake Jars 94
    Blackberry Drizzle Muffins 93
    Blackberry Jam 88
    Bread 86
    Cheese Scones 97
    Sausage and Caramelised Onion Plaits 101
    Strawberry Basket Cakes 98
pies:
    Apple, Blackberry and Plum Pie 167
    Chocolate Orange Whoopie Pies 148
    Mince Pies 185
plums 167
pork 101
'Pretty as a Picture' Mother's Day Biscuits 32
primrose petals:

Crystallised Rose Petals and Flowers 24
where to buy 225
see also edible flowers and leaves
pumpkin 154

R
raspberries:
    Mini Raspberry, Lemon and Chocolate Éclairs 115
    Raspberry Iced Bunny Biscuits 54
    Raspberry Iced Tea 112
    White Chocolate, Raspberry and Rose Petal Cake 25
Raspberry Iced Bunny Biscuits 54
Raspberry Iced Tea 112
Red Velvet Angel Cupcakes 190
Red Velvet Cupcake Ice Cream 202
resources, directory of 225–6
rose petals:
    Crystallised Rose Petals and Flowers 24
    Fresh Floral Ice Cubes 114
    Rose Petal Jam 107
    where to buy 225
    White Chocolate, Raspberry and Rose Petal Cake 25
Rose Petal Jam 107
Rosy Teacup Cupcakes 108

S
Salted Caramel Peanut Butter Cups 201
Sausage and Caramelised Onion Plaits 101
Scones (sweet) 131
    see also Cheese Scones
Shirt and Tie Biscuits 136
shops and suppliers 225–6
Snowflake Biscuits 198
soft drinks:
    Blackberry Cordial 91
    Homemade Lemonade 72
    Mulled Apple Juice *see* Mulled Cider
    Raspberry Iced Tea 112

Spiced Pumpkin Bundt Cake 154
Stained Glass Window Biscuits 180
Sticky Toffee Puddings 164
strawberries:
    Fresh Strawberry Ice Cream 66
    Mini Strawberries and Cream Cupcakes 124
    Strawberry Basket Cakes 98
    Strawberry Jam 74
Strawberry Basket Cakes 98
Strawberry Jam 74
suppliers 225–6

T
toffee:
    Sticky Toffee Puddings 164
    Toffee Apple Cupcakes 151
    Toffee Apple Jam 150
Toffee Apple Cupcakes 151
Toffee Apple Jam 150
toffee apples 147
Two-tiered Celebration Cake 104

V
Valentine's Day-themed recipes:
    as gifts 216
    Heart-Shaped Ombré Ruffle Cake 210
    Lollipop Biscuits 216
    Mini Red Velvet Heart Cakes 213
viola petals:
    Crystallised Rose Petals and Flowers 24
    where to buy 225
    see also edible flowers and leaves

W
White Chocolate Chip Cookies 79
White Chocolate, Raspberry and Rose Petal Cake 25

ACKNOWLEDGEMENTS

I have so many people to thank for their help but firstly, I would like to thank John Blake Publishing for giving me the chance to publish this, my first cook book, at my young age of sixteen, especially Toby Buchan, Anna Marx and Stuart Finglass for their kind and wonderful support and for believing in me. Thank you so much.

Thank you to Express Newspapers for their fantastic support.

Thank you also to Graeme and Laura, who worked hard to help me achieve the design I envisaged and helped produce a beautiful book.

A huge thank you to Joanna Henderson for taking the wonderful photographs of my recipes, and to Charlotte Love who sourced the perfect props and helped style my recipes so beautifully. We all had a busy, fun and exciting time together.

And thanks must also go to my fantastic friends and family who have enthusiastically tasted my recipes.

Finally, my special thanks to my mum, dad and sister for their love and support, especially my mum who inspired me to cook and bake and to write my first cook book.